Bicentennial
Bike Tours

Recycle the past with 200 historical
rides and 100 maps, prompted by the
200th birthday celebration of the
United States.

GOUSHĀ PUBLICATIONS
San Jose, California

Editor: **Marian May**
Designer: **Roger Waterman**
Cover Illustration: **Masami Miyamoto**
Editorial Assistants: **Steve Webber**
Dianna Yee

We are indebted to the League of American Wheelmen and the following expert cyclists for tour routes and definitive notes:

Wayne Alfred	William Hoffman
Hartley Alley	Keith Kingbay
John Boettger	Therese Lepine
Joe Bowen	Horace Marshall
Sam Braxton	Lowell Mason
Shirley Braxton	Chick Mead
Keith Cottam	James O'Leary
Donald Darling	Tom Owen
John D'Angelo	Carroll Quimby
James Farnsworth	Roland Rich
Clifford Franz	Paul Schwemler
Floyd Frazine	S. Arnold Shields
Joel Glazer	Mrs. Thomas Steffan
Fred Gooding	Joyce Sulanke
Ray Guest	John Vanderpoel
Phyllis Harmon	Jeannette Westin
Warren Hinterland	William Woods

Photos: Malcolm Anderson, 48, 58, 112, 136, 205. Florida News Bureau, 78. Robert Iacopi, 31, 119, 147, 149, 184, 193. Schwinn Bicycle Co., 47, 103, 169, 207. Steve Webber, 5, 6, 32, 43, 45, 51, 93, 105, 164, 175, 179.

ISBN No. 0-913040-20-7
Library of Congress No. 72-97827

Printed in the United States
First edition 1973
First printing April 1973

Contents

How to Use "Bicentennial Bike Tours"

Bicentennial Bike Tours invites the growing legions of cyclists to board bikes and recycle the past. Prompted by the 1976 Bicentennial celebration of the United States and the amazing popularity of bicycling, this collection of tours puts your wheels straight on the path to history across the nation. Part of the Lewis and Clark trail is followed, the 200-year-old Spanish background of California is explored. You will cycle to the spots where Washington made his Delaware crossing and Paul Revere rode to warn the Colonists.

A bike can put you into areas that you either could not or would not see from an automobile. You get right into the midst of things. This is especially true on such trips as those in **Bicentennial Bike Tours.**

This book won't tell you how to buy a bike or how to fix one. It won't tell you how to get in shape for a hard ride. It is simply a "where to" book, leaving all the " how to" to the dozens of excellent books and periodicals that cover those phases of bicycling.

What the Tours Include

Check the index for historical points of interest. There are fascinating places to visit, all of which had a part in the development of the country. There are one hundred basic tours, each with its own adjacent, detailed map. Each basic tour not only reveals the history of the area but also indicates resting places, accommodations or campgrounds and eating spots. In addition, there are at least a hundred more loops, optionals and side trips.

About the Maps

All of the maps were specially prepared just for this tour book. An attempt was made to pare away all unnecessary material and leave only the important points, including major access roads and nearby cities. The basic route is often a loop, sometimes just a one-way run. In tricky areas of a tour, detailed road-by-road descriptions are given in addition to the maps.

Every one of the tours in this book

has been covered by a skilled rider. In all, around forty expert cyclists reported bike routes and additional information.

Above every map is a block of related information: approximate mileage, best times to tour, conditions of the terrain, traffic to expect, as well as the historical spots.

On any tour it is a good idea to obtain local maps when possible. Do not hesitate to ask directions along the way. (At the time of printing all maps and information in **Bicentennial Bike Tours** had been carefully checked and assumed correct. But the scene does change, so check ahead when in doubt.)

Tailoring the Tours

Use **Bicentennial Bike Tours** for planning lengthy bike camping trips if you are a cyclist looking for 200-mile runs to cloud reaching altitudes. If you are a weekend rider, refer to it for historic one-day junkets in your own area or in a combination automobile-bicycle vacation where you can drive within miles of the destination and experience part of the trip with an enjoyment only bike touring can bring.

Bikes have a lot of plus features. Early in their popularity, in the mid-1800's, they got a huge number of people off their horses (some alarmists even declared that walking would soon be obsolete). No modern cyclist needs to be reminded of the ecological role of the bike—the worthy feature of not further polluting the air. An additional attraction is a kind of personal ecology —a healthy heart in a healthy body, and a happy panacea for the strains of modern life.

In reporting a tour of Yellowstone, one of the experts who contributed to the book told this story. "When we arrived at Horse Creek Campground, there was a huge self-contained camper in the parking lot. As we were setting up our little camp the owners came to visit. As they left they said, 'You know, when we saw you pedal up we felt so sorry for you. But as we talk to you and hear what all you have done and seen, we feel sorry not for you but for ourselves. You are having a much greater experience than either my wife or myself.'" And that is what bike touring is all about.

New England

A Northern Maine Century Challenge

A challenging ride through the hills of Maine, this tour is recommended only for cyclists who are in excellent condition. The trip covers over 100 miles from near the Canadian border at Jackman to Waterville in the southern part of the Pine Tree State. (There is a chance for a ride into Canada. An optional trip north to Quebec is about 100 miles, one way.)

From Jackman the route heads south on U.S. 201. Continue the tour past Lake Parlin to where the road begins to follow Kennebec River.

The Kennebec has been extremely important in the development and history of Maine. To the Indian, the Manitou Kennebec (river-god) was not only a highway and source of food; at times it was a wrathful idol that crushed canoes and swallowed its victims as it swept entire villages away when in flood. To the early traders it opened up the wealth of furs and fish in the Kennebec Valley and later carried the logs for the lucrative lumber business in Augusta.

The route follows the river past Moscow to Bingham. The town was named after William Bingham, a wealthy Philadelphia banker who bought 2 million acres around the area.

About eight miles south is Solon. Some interesting sights here include, Caratunk Falls, rare Indian carvings on nearby rock ledges and Arnold's Landing.

Benedict Arnold, famed for spilling the beans during the Revolution, managed to keep them on his plate over campfires along this same route you're traveling. At Solon is an Arnold Trail Marker with a tablet commemorating this as the spot where Arnold and his army landed October 7, 1775, remaining overnight prior to the carry around Caratunk Falls.

Still further south in Skowhegan (Indian for "place to watch the fish") are some fine restaurants. O'Solo Mio

Approximate mileage: 104, one way; 100 more to Quebec, Canada.

Best times for touring: Summer months.

Terrain: Very hilly over excellent roads.

Traffic: During the summer the traffic can be heavy as this route is the most direct between Quebec and New England.

Historical points of interest: Benedict Arnold's landing at Solon, Old Fort Halifax.

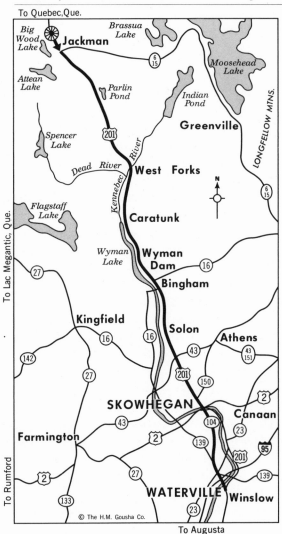

is especially recommended to cyclists. From here the route changes to State 104. Follow this road to State 139 which will take you into Waterville.

Once the site of a large Indian village, Waterville is now an important industrial city. Points of interest here are Colby College, founded in 1818, the Bixler Art and Music Center with American and European exhibits, and Old Fort Halifax.

The fort, located 1 mile east on the bank of the Kennebec River, formed the northernmost line of English defense on the river. Although strategically located in the midst of important Indian travel routes along the river the fort was never attacked. All that remains, after it was dismantled in 1763, is one blockhouse. Nearby is an excellent view of Ticonic Falls from the bridge over the Kennebec.

Action Packed Sprint to the Coast of Maine

From a fresh water lake in New Hampshire this 80-mile run heads out to the famous salty coast of Maine. Along the way, museums, art colonies and New England scenery add something special.

The tour begins near the banks of Lake Winnipesaukee in the summer resort town of Alton. Ride State 11 out of town heading southeast towards the Atlantic.

Just a little off the route at Farmington is where the Nordica Homestead Museum has mementos of the famous opera star, Lillian Nordica, who was born in the town. Also near Farmington watch for signs to the Schuller Museum. The museum has a fascinating collection of 14th to 17th century European and Japanese arms.

Bicycling east on State 16 bypass is allowed. You ride on limited access road about a mile to pick up U.S. 202 to Sanford, Maine. Continue past Sanford to Alfred where the tour picks up State 111. Follow the signs for the county road turnoff to Kennebunkport and the beaches of the coast of Maine.

The Seashore Trolley Museum is a favorite with visitors to the city. Nearly 90 antique streetcars from the U.S. and abroad are on display. Trolley rides are given during the summer.

Continue down State 9 along the coast to Ogunquit. Here Maine's "stern and rockbound coast" becomes a long, sandy, salty stretch of beach. Along the Marginal Way, paths through the cliffs offer beautiful ocean vistas.

The picturesque harbor of Perkins Cove has attracted a large art colony. Galleries include: Museum of Art of Ogunquit, American sculpture and paintings; Barn Gallery, local works, concerts, lectures; Ogunquit Art Center, work from all over the country by leading artists.

Down U.S. 1 from Ogunquit the route runs into an area known as the

Approximate mileage: 80, one way.

Best times for touring: Summer.

Terrain: Unusually flat for New England; minimal hills.

Traffic: Tourist traffic everywhere. Riding east on State 16 bypass is allowed for a mile.

Historical points of interest: Schuller Museum, Trolley Museum, Lady Pepperrell House, Fort McClary Memorial.

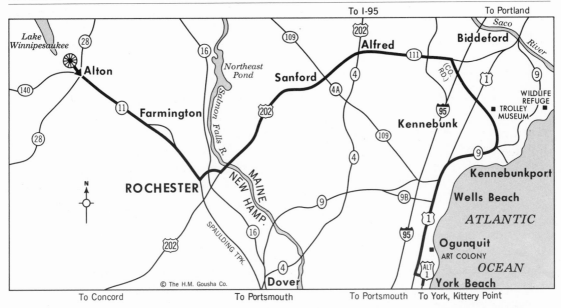

Yorks. York Village, a haven of Colonial atmosphere, was the nation's first city with a charter. The Old Gaol which is open to visitors, is believed to be the oldest remaining public building (1653) of the English colonies. The First Parish Church is the first church built in the colonies after that of Jamestown, Virginia. Other interesting structures include: the Wildox House, Jefferds' Tavern, the Old School House and the Elizabeth Perkins House.

The tour picks up State Route 103 to Kittery Point and Fort McClary Memorial. A restored blockhouse stands on the site of the old fort built in 1809.

The Lady Pepperrell House is also located nearby. Built for the widow of Sir William Pepperrell, a soldier-merchant made a baronet before the Revolution, the house is a Georgian structure of unusual elaborateness.

On a tour like this, every place you look is a good resting spot. Motels are abundant. Don't expect to camp.

Old Man of the Mountains Spectacular

Covered bridges, craggy mountains and a famous profile combine to make this 100-mile loop through New Hampshire's White Mountains a unique cycling excursion.

Head east on State 112 up over the Kancamagus. The climb is steep for 11 miles so use low gears or walk.

Continue along the route past Passaconaway to the visitor center. From here you can take a shortcut up the road cutting 20 miles off the loop. Be forewarned—it's tough.

On the main tour continue along State 112 heading into Conway. Near town you will find two covered bridges, relics from another era. If bridges don't excite you continue on to North Conway and head up Cranmore Mountain. This is the jumpoff point for the famous Skimobile. Built in 1938, this is a forerunner of modern ski lifts.

The next stop could be a barbecue or good night's rest; both available at Echo Lake Campground a few miles north on State 16. This entire route abounds in facilities.

The tour follows the Saco River and picks up U.S. 302 heading into the heart of notch land. The route will continue on the highway north past the Crawford Notch, an enormous landslide scar from the continental ice sheet. Near here the Mt. Washington Cog Railroad, the first mountain-climbing cog railway in the world, winds its way, in a three hour journey to the top of the looming mountain.

The tour picks up U.S. 3, passing Profile Lake and the "Old Man of the Mountains," a rock profile formation that inspired a story by Nathaniel Hawthorne called *The Great Stone Face.* Also along the route is the Basin, a granite pothole 20 feet deep eroded over the years by a waterfall.

The Flume, a natural chasm 800 feet long, and Indian Head are the last of the natural wonders as you head back.

Approximate mileage: 100

Best times for touring: Avoid holidays, fall weekends and winter.

Terrain: Steep uphill climbs that lead to spectacular drops.
Ride tour counter clockwise.

Traffic: Not bad except on holidays; autumn leaf-looking time.

Historical points of interest: Covered bridges, The Great Stone Face, Cog Railroad.

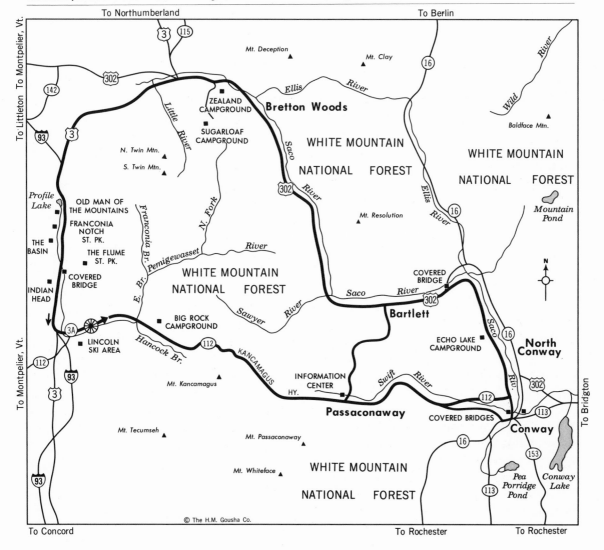

© The H.M. Gousha Co.

Lakeside Challenge Around Winnipesaukee

This 63-mile tour through the rolling hills of New Hampshire circles Lake Winnipesaukee. It is a challenging ride even for cyclists with low-geared bikes and strong legs but the scenery is worth the effort.

The tour begins at Weirs Beach off U.S. 3. This is a popular recreational area and is the scene of much activity in the summer when regattas are held.

At the southern end of Weirs is a stone causeway leading out to a granite canopy that houses Endicott Rock. It is believed early explorers to the area carved the initials of Governor John Endicott of the Massachusetts Bay Colony on the rock to claim the territory.

The route heads north on U.S. 3 to Meredith. A favorite water sports center, this town also has the Meredith Auto Museum with antique cars.

A few miles past Meredith the tour takes State Route 25B across the upper edge of Lake Winnipesaukee to Moultonborough. The Old Country Store nearby is an interesting excursion into the past.

Now pick up State Route 109 heading south. This long run, without any large towns, offers many scenic views of the lake. Stop at Libby Museum to see the nature collection, Indian relics.

The largest town on the lake is the resort community of Wolfeboro. Heralded as the first vacation spot in the United States it is the site of the first true "summer" home, built by Governor Sir John Wentworth in the early 1800's.

Other sights are the Wolfeboro Arts and Crafts Center where handicrafts made throughout the state are exhibited and sold.

The tour continues on to South Wolfeboro where it picks up State Route 28. Be sure to take the State 28A cutoff to Alton Bay. Cyclists often miss it. At the junction with State Route 11 head north and back to the departure point at Weirs Beach.

Approx. mileage: 63.

Best times for touring: Spring or fall.

Terrain: Some pretty steep climbs, hilly lakeside roads.

Traffic: Heaviest traffic on State Route 25.

Historical points of interest: Endicott Rock, Meredith Auto Museum, Wolfeboro.

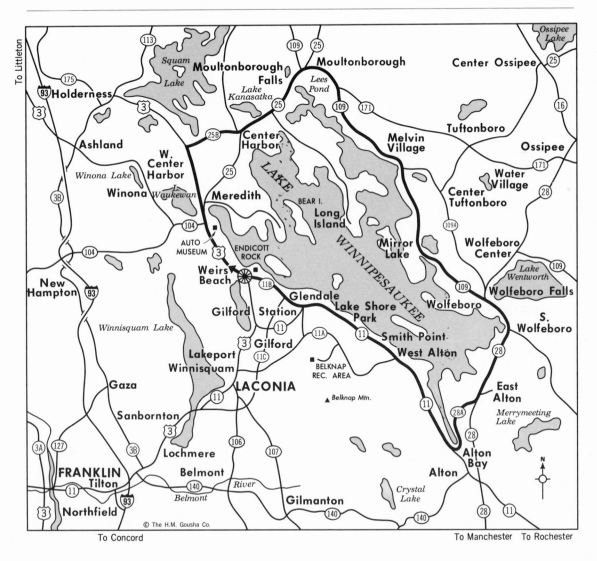

Covered Bridges and Maple Sugar in Vermont

Lots of quiet Vermont history, sugar making, a museum or two, and perhaps a lazy picnic by a New England pond set the mood for this leisurely tour through the verdant countryside. The loop can be easily ridden in one day, with enough spare time for sightseeing.

Adequate bike shops are a rarity; plan to carry spare parts and tools for minor repairs.

As for lodging, ask about "guest homes", they're clean and quaint and rooms are available for $5. Food is easy to find, larger towns will have small restaurants and even the smallest hamlet will have a country store where a lunch of fruit, cheese will fill your saddle bags.

The tour begins in St. Johnsbury off U.S. 5. A favorite stopping place of visitors to this beautiful town is the Maple Museum. Here at the Old Sugar House you can witness maple syrup production; also a museum and films. At the Maple Grove candy factory, tours leave every ten minutes Monday through Friday. Free.

Art lovers will appreciate the St. Johnsbury Athenaeum where artists from the Hudson River school along with European masterpieces are on display.

Fairbanks Museum of Natural Science and Planetarium, named after Thaddeus Fairbanks, who invented the platform scale in the city in 1830, contains a collection of Polynesian and African arts.

The bike route heads south along U.S. 5 through Passumpsic to Barnet and East Ryegate. The latter two towns share the distinction of being the only two villages in Vermont founded by colonists from across the Atlantic.

In this area keep a lookout for interesting old graveyards. If you are a buff, you are in marvelous tombstone-rubbing country.

Head north to Peacham and take a look around here for the town post

Approximate mileage: 35. Optional sidetrip, 20.

Best times for touring: Memorial Day and Halloween.

Terrain: Moderate hills, few steep grades.

Traffic: No problem, but ride with caution.

Historical points of interest: St. Johnsbury, Crossroads Bank, Maple Grove Plant, Fairbanks Museum of Natural Science, the Athenaeum.

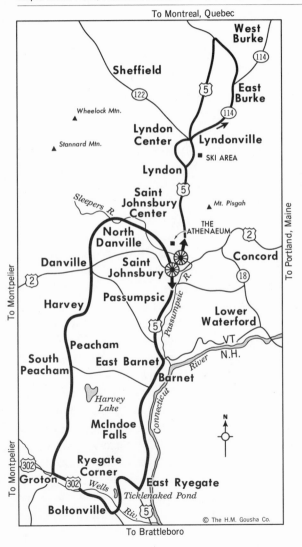

office, a charming and unusual edifice. Oliver Johnson, the influential editor of the *Anti-Slavery Standard,* learned the printing trade in this town.

Past Harvey the route bounces along through New England countryside to Danville, the home of what is called the country's biggest crossroads bank. In 1952 the Wall Street Journal wrote a story on this little community bank under a headline that read: "Biggest Crossroads Bank Thrives on Cattle Loans Competitors Don't Want." The Caledonia National Bank was founded in 1825.

The tour loops back to St. Johnsbury where an optional sidetrip picks up U.S. 5 north through the ski areas around Lyndon and East Burke. There are five covered bridges in and about the area if you fancy such structures and have enough energy to make this final bridge-on-the-river try.

Back Road Loop to Hubbardton Battlefield

Famous names and places abound on this scenic loop on Vermont's back roads. Motel accommodations are good. There are also state parks for camping and lakes for swimming along the route.

Up the line a short sprint from the starting place in Center Rutland watch for signs leading to Wilson Castle. Here sixteen buildings are furnished in regal elegance. Royal tariff: about $2.

Along here you will ride by the world's deepest marble quarries. A few miles further up the road is Proctor and just outside of town, the Vermont Marble Company. Exhibits include a carving of the "Last Supper" from a solid block of marble, the Gallery of Presidents and bas-reliefs of many of our country's leaders.

Next stop is Brandon, a resort and residential town that is the birthplace of the "Little Giant," Lincoln's nemesis Stephen A. Douglas. The cottage where he was born is at the entrance of the town.

Pick up State Route 73 to the junction at State Route 30 and head south through Sudbury to Hubbardton.

The only battle of the Revolution which took place entirely on Vermont soil was fought just out of town. The Hubbardton Battle Monument and Museum commemorates the event. Displayed in the museum is a diorama of the early stages of the struggle and a large, animated relief map with a running commentary of the battle.

The route continues down State 30 to Lake Bomoseen. Fishing, swimming and picnicking along with overnight camping are some of the attractions of Bomoseen State Park.

At the junction of U.S. 4 a few miles south, an optional sidetrip continues down State 30 to Poultney, looping through Middleton Springs and Pawlet. The 25-mile loop is rich in history. Pawlet was the spot where in 1777 Herrick's Rangers, later known as the Terror of the Tories, was founded. East

Approximate mileage: 35, with 25 mile optional sidetrip.

Best times for touring: Spring or fall.

Terrain: Mostly back roads; grades not difficult.

Traffic: Not bad.

Historical points of interest: Vermont Marble Exhibit, Wilson Castle, Hubbardton Battlefield, Pawlet, Poultney.

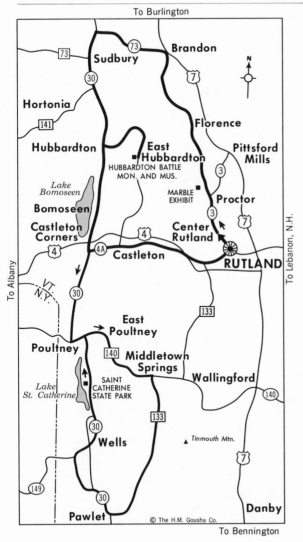

Poultney is where famous newsman Horace Greeley and Raymond Jones learned the printing trade. At the nearby Two Editors Inn, named for the mighty penmen, you can warm up for the rest of the journey. Back in Revolutionary times a famous toast was given in the town. Captain William Watson, obviously an outspoken chap, shouted, "To the enemies of our country." Then added, "May they have cobweb breeches, a porcupine saddle, a hard trotting horse and an eternal journey."

The main route takes State 4A to Castleton. At Zadock Remington's Tavern Ethan Allen, Seth Warner and their famous "Green Mountain Boys" planned the successful attacks on Fort Ticonderoga and Crown Point.

A Heritage Trail in The Green Mountains

An important Revolutionary War battlefield, museums, and quaint New England towns mark this rugged 160-mile jaunt up the middle of Vermont—an excellent cycling adventure with hostels and camping facilities.

Begin in Brattleboro with plans to be picked up in Montpelier a few days later. Ride two miles south of the city and take a look at Fort Dummer, the first settlement in Vermont, founded in 1724.

When you reach the junction of State 9 and State 100 you can vote for an interesting optional trip to the Bennington Battle site, about 20 miles away. Here untrained American militia managed to overcome the British forces of General Burgoyne, who was later defeated at Saratoga. Much earlier the Vermont militia was involved in a territorial skirmish with New York. New York was trying to claim the land in this area and the militia drove the New Yorkers back. To the locals the militia was called the "Green Mountain Boys"; to New Yorkers they were the "Bennington Mob." Some interesting stops here are a monument to commemorate the victory over Burgoyne, the Bennington Museum, and the Bennington Gallery.

Back on the main route, head north on State 100 into the Green Mountain National Forest, passing numerous ski slopes. The grades are steep and you will work hard.

Coming into Weston is a trip into the past. The town dates from the 18th century and many of the buildings have been restored. Farrar-Mansur House, an old tavern established in 1797, has been renewed to its original condition and now serves as a museum and community house. Visit Vermont Country Store to see an authentic display of early wares. Weston is also the home of the famed Guild of Old Time Crafts and Industries.

Skirting the Green Mountain Na-

Approximate mileage: 150 one way; 40 mile round trip optional to Bennington.

Best times for touring: Impossible in winter, choose warmer times of the year.

Terrain: Steep grades in the Green Mountains.

Traffic: Congested near cities; use caution on State 100 at all times.

Historical points of interest: Fort Dummer, Bennington Battlefield, Weston restorations, Montpelier.

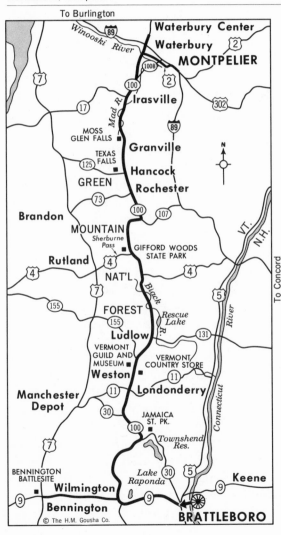

tional Forest, the route now runs along the Black and the Mad Rivers. Continuing on State 100, you will enter Rochester. Here there is a beautiful white church with graceful spires. In 1907 Rochester was awarded the prize as the model town of the United States.

A few miles north of Rochester is Moss Glen Falls, and a few miles west on State Route 125 is Texas Falls.

Before entering Irasville the foothills become somewhat barren. The Mad River which parallels the road becomes thinner, with the banks lined with trees. Irasville itself is a town that is relatively secluded from bus lines.

At this point a 20 mile side trip to Montpelier heads east on U.S. Route 2. The city is the state capital and the State House, built in 1859, is constructed of Vermont granite with the dome covered with gold leaf. Also here is the Kent Museum, the Vermont State Library, the Supreme Court.

The tour ends in Waterbury Center which is two miles past the intersection of State Route 100 and Interstate 89. Hostel accommodations here.

Revolutionary Ride With Paul Revere

The shot heard 'round the world still echoes through the historical landmarks that dot this Massachusetts loop tour. The towns of Lexington and Concord are historical legends and the spawning ground for such revolutionary heroes as the Minutemen and Paul Revere.

On this ride the cyclist will retrace part of the route where Revere galloped to warn the colonists that "the British are coming." The starting point for the tour is Lexington which can be reached via State Route 4/225. Leave your car at the Lexington Green, the site of the first skirmish of the Revolutionary War. The Minuteman statue commemorates the small force of men who refused the British command to disperse and began the fight for freedom. Eight Americans, the first war casualties, died here. Also on the green is Buckman Tavern.

Going west from Lexington on State 2A the cyclist will pass the Minuteman National Historical Park. Nearby is the place where Paul Revere was captured by the British. Riding with him at the time were two other colonials, William Dawes and Doctor Sam Prescott. Revere and Dawes were captured, but Prescott made it to Concord with the warning.

Just outside Concord is the Alcott House, home of Louisa May Alcott, author of *Little Women*. The house was later bought in 1852 by Nathaniel Hawthorne. Another literary figure whose home is preserved nearby is Ralph Waldo Emerson. Concord's Antiquarian House, at Turnpike and Lexington Road, displays a reconstruction of Emerson's study.

At the Concord Bridge the British met a determined band of several hundred Minutemen, who had been summoned by clanging churchbells. Emerson immortalized the scene in verse.

The tour continues from here along Monument Street, River Road and Hwy. 225 through the town of Bedford and back through lovely New England countryside to Lexington.

Approx. mileage: 17.

Best times for touring: Anytime except winter.

Terrain: Moderate grades on asphalt roads.

Traffic: Average traffic is light; heavy at commute hours near Hanscom Field road.

Historical points of interest: The towns of Lexington and Concord, Minuteman National Historical Park, Alcott House, Emerson House, Concord Antiquarian Society, and Minuteman statues.

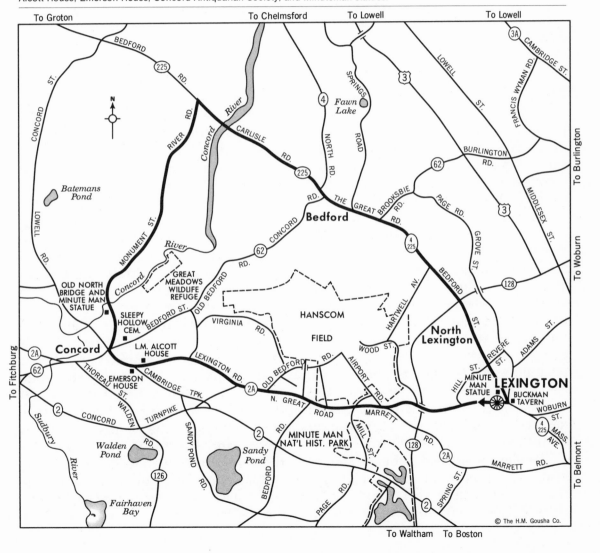

Province Lands—the Untouched Cape Cod

Eight miles through the Cape Cod National Seashore offers the cyclist a glimpse of the famed and varied Maine coastline. Forests, ponds, bogs and giant dunes make this tour a seashore spectacular. The entire area, backyard to the art colony of Provincetown, was set aside as early as 1670 in pioneering conservation action by the "Plimoth Colony."

The trail begins at the Beech Forest Parking area. Proceed westerly through a densely wooded area dotted with fresh water ponds and marshes. As the trail curves to the left, away from the Great Pond complex, you will enter a pitch pine woods. The trees here, black oak, sassafras and pitch pine owe their existence to the repeated forest fires in the area. The trees sprout profusely from the roots of those destroyed.

The short spur road to Bennett Pond leads to a quiet and graceful grouping of trees; a nice spot for a picnic.

Back on the route you will pass again through forest until just east of Pasture Pond where the trail breaks open to the impressive sight of the Province Lands sand dunes. Off in the distance to the north, past Hatches Harbor, the Race Point Lighthouse, dunes and scattered pines, lies the Atlantic Ocean.

The trail continues through dunes, under Province Lands Rd. and left to Herring Cove Beach. After a rest in this quiet, scenic place retrace the tour to the intersection of the main trail and the Herring Cove spur.

A new plant community is apparent now as you ride northeast through the cranberry bogs. A jumbled assortment of native pitch pine is mixed with exotic pines in an effort to arrest the gradual drift of the sand dunes. Soon another spur cuts off to the right for the Province Lands Visitor Center where detailed information is available.

Race Point Beach on the Atlantic deserves a leisurely stop before backtracking the trail to Beech Forest.

Approximate mileage: 8.

Best times for touring: Any season except winter.

Terrain: Paved trail through forests, past ponds, bogs and giant dunes.

Traffic: None.

Historical points of interest: Province Lands, set aside as early as 1670 by the "Plimoth Colony" in pioneering conservation action.

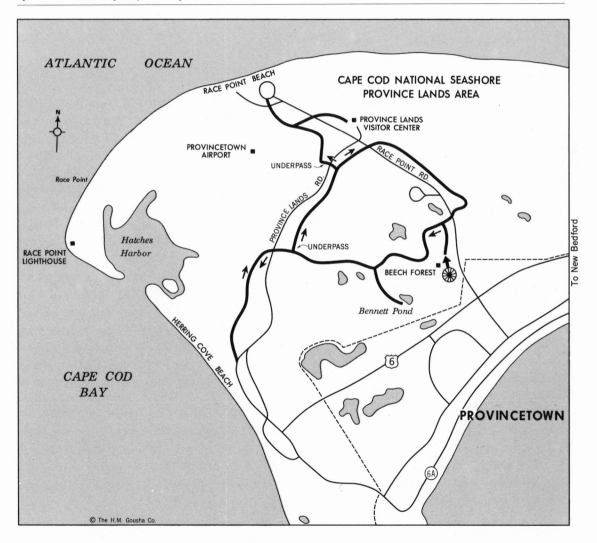

Double Century Circle around Rhode Island

Rhode Island may be the smallest state in the union but for cycling fun it ranks right up there with the big boys. This 200-mile tour through famous port towns is of special interest because the route circles the entire state.

Fill up with a little Providence history before you start. Founded in 1636 by Roger Williams, Providence is a gracious mixture of modern and traditional. The John Brown House described by John Quincy Adams as "the most magnificent and elegant mansion I have ever seen on this continent," is the home of the Rhode Island Historical Society.

The tour heads north past Pawtucket. Stop at the Old Slater Mill Museum (1793) for a look at the cradle of the textile industry in America.

Continue north to Woonsocket, then south to the Scituate Reservoir. Ride south out to the ocean and follow the water around to the Jamestown bridge. Cross over and circle the island. There is a camping area in the southern part of the town. The Old Windmill, (1787) is an interesting place to visit before crossing the Newport Bridge. You'll have to pay $2 and walk your bike.

The first Quakers to come to the New World settled in Newport in 1657 about ten years after the city was founded by a group fleeing the religious intolerance of Massachusetts.

During the Revolution, Newport put up a gallant struggle, burning one British ship and firing on others before the Redcoats landed 9,000 men and captured the city.

Many magnificent old homes trace the history of this elegant area—The Breakers, The Elms, and Belcourt Castle. Also, Touro Synagogue (1763) is the oldest in America.

Continuing north, Portsmouth is the site of Butts Hill Fort where the only land battle in Rhode Island during the Revolution was fought.

An optional tour circles Tiverton, Little Compton and Bristol.

Approximate mileage: 200.

Best times for touring: Late spring or early summer when prevailing winds are southwest and offshore.

Terrain: Good secondary roads.

Traffic: Heavy in cities, tourist areas.

Historical points of interest: Old States Mill, Newport houses, Providence, Jamestown.

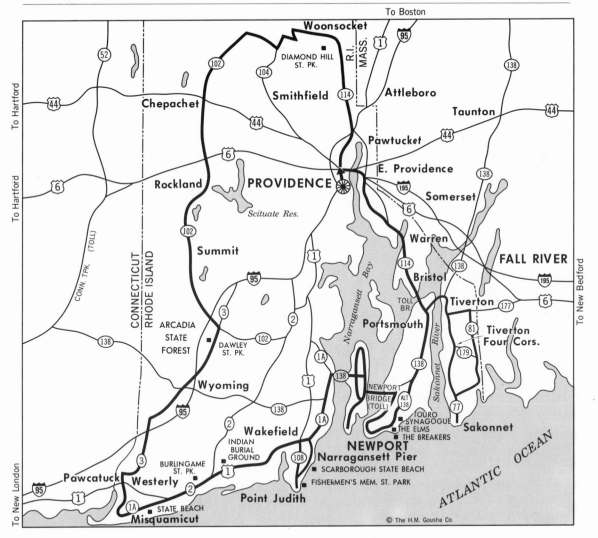

Through Quiet Hills to Colonial Newgate Prison

Quiet hills, secluded lakes and lovely old towns make Connecticut a haven for the cyclist who likes to take his rides with a grain of tranquility. The three hills involved should not require walking.

The tour begins in Windsor Locks, accessible via Interstate 91. Although rail service is available, it is unlikely you could get your bike on the train—no baggage cars.

Before heading out there is an enjoyable optional sidetrip to Warehouse Point and the Trolley Museum.

Leave Windsor Locks via Spring St. At the junction of State Route 75 is the Bradley Air Museum. Besides displaying the famous fighter planes built and used during the last 30 years the museum contains such oddities as Silas Brooks' balloon "Jupiter" (1886).

To avoid State 20 traffic on a busy stretch, continue along State 75 to Poquonock. From here pick up Rainbow Road and head northwest. Follow State 20 through East Granby to the top of Turkey Hill (a rest stop) and turn right onto Newgate Road. Head up the hill one mile to the Old Newgate Prison.

This ancient copper mine served as a prison for Colonial felons and political prisoners during the Revolution. Its huge pervading walls loom over the damp underground cells that remain virtually the same today as when they were occupied two centuries ago. The gatehouse has many displays reflecting Newgate's history.

Continue down the road to the bottom of the hill and turn left. Take the second right and then another right about a mile later, under a trestle.

At the four-way intersection, turn left to State 190 and ride between the Congamond Lakes into Massachusetts.

The tour takes Sheep Pasture Road right to the end and heads right back to State 190. Here head left into Suffield. Visit the Hathaway House (1760) before taking State 75 to Suffield Street.

Approximate mileage: 30.

Best times for touring: May to October.

Terrain: Easy ride, even for children. Only three hills of consequence.

Traffic: Light.

Historical points of interest: Newgate Prison, Bradley Air Museum, Trolley Museum, Hathaway House.

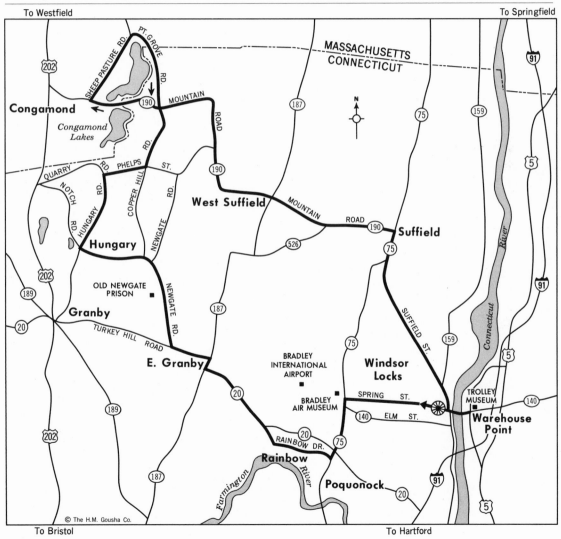

Dinosaur Tracks Along the Connecticut River

Picturesque Connecticut is the site of this 50-mile loop tour that features dinosaurs, an opera house and a castle.

The tour begins at Rocky Hill off Interstate 91. The outskirts of the town is a place where dinosaurs once walked—Dinosaur State Park. Here you can stand on a deck and look down on monstrous tracks embedded in the valley floor, left by these behemoths who roamed 180 million years ago.

To get back into modern history, take the ferry across the Connecticut River out of Rocky Hill and pick up State 160 until the junction at State Route 17 in South Glastonbury. Turn right and go south to State Route 66. Turn left to State Route 151 and head south to State Route 149 and follow this road to East Haddam.

East Haddam has a varied blend of sightseeing pleasures. For music lovers the Goodspeed Opera House should strike a nostalgic chord. Built in 1876 the multi-storied building has been restored and now is the site of summer musicals. During the rest of the year travelogues, concerts and special productions are presented.

And something for you space age folks—the Connecticut Yankee Atomic Power Company. Guided tours explain such mysteries as nuclear power; closed circuit TV reveals the control room; also films and lectures. A treat for American history buffs—the Nathan Hale Schoolhouse where the courageous "Martyr of the Revolution" taught school over 200 years ago is a proud landmark of the city.

Out of East Haddam cross the Connecticut River, this time via a bridge, and take a right at State 99. Continue to State 148 where you will make another ferry crossing over to Hadlyme. For those who dream of castles in the air, this area should suit your fantasy. The Gillette Castle State Park, across the river, conjures up a true life castle built by actor William Gillette. The structure

Approximate mileage: 50.

Best times for touring: April 15 to October 15.

Terrain: Rolling hills; some steep grades.

Traffic: Heavy near towns and tourist areas.

Historical points of interest: Dinosaur Park, Goodspeed Opera House, Nathan Hale Schoolhouse, Connecticut Yankee Atomic Power, Gillette Castle.

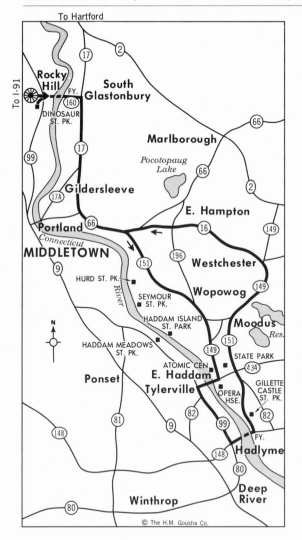

is of medieval Rhenish design. Tours from Memorial Day to Columbus Day. Admission.

Continue north on State 82 to State 151. From here follow the road north to the town of Moodus. The tour then takes State 149 out of the town to State 16. Head left on State 16 and continue on to Cobalt and the junction of State 66.

From here the tour begins to retrace itself back to the departure point at Rocky Hill. The last adventure before resting your tired muscles is another quiet ferry boat ride across the Connecticut River.

New York-Pennsylvania

Two Part Parallel of the Old Erie Canal

The Old Erie Canal parallels most of this 165 mile tour through upper state New York. The ride is broken up into two parts, both heading out from Rochester. The trip to Syracuse is about 90 miles; the ride to Niagara Falls around 75.

The city of Rochester sprang up around flour mills that were operated by falls in the Genessee River. The town would have remained a small affair if not for the Erie Canal.

Governor Dewitt Clinton had struggled for fifteen years to build the canal against powerful opposition. Using locks to raise the water over the natural terrain, the digging continued until 1825 when Clinton boarded a barge in Buffalo and traveled entirely by water to New York. The price of moving a ton of freight between Buffalo and Albany soon dropped from $100 to $10 and little towns like Buffalo, Rochester and Syracuse became important.

Shutter bugs will love Rochester for this is the home of Eastman Kodak and guided tours of three different plants are offered. The George Eastman House, home of the man who produced the first modern portable roll film camera, is now a free museum.

Take State 31 east out of the city along the old canal through Newark. At Weedsport, turn on to State 31B and then onto State 5 into Syracuse.

Syracuse is a product of salt and the Erie Canal. A great salt deposit was known to be there from colonial times but there was no economical way to transport it. The canal paved the way.

The other tour from Rochester takes State 31 west through Lockport to Niagara Falls. At Lockport you can witness one of the great engineering feats of the time. The land drops from the high Niagara escarpment to the plains below. Five great locks were built here to rise and lower the shipping.

Everyone knows about Niagara Falls—honeymoon destination.

Approximate mileage: 165 total; Rochester to Syracuse-90; Rochester to Niagara-75.

Best times for touring: Spring, summer or fall.

Terrain: Relatively flat, rolling country in some parts.

Traffic: Congested in large cities.

Historical points of interest: The Old Erie Canal, Syracuse, Lockport.

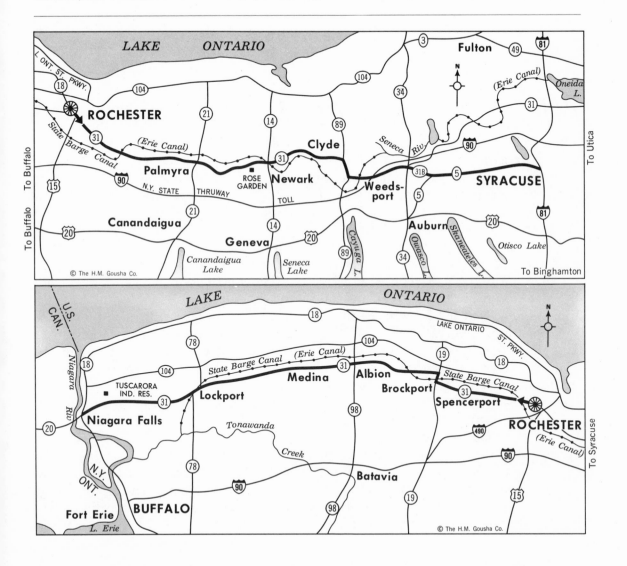

© The H.M. Gousha Co.

© The H.M. Gousha Co.

Turning Point Tour to Saratoga Battlefield

The Battle at Saratoga in 1777 was the turning point of the Revolutionary War. The Americans, under Gen. Horatio Gates, defeated "Gentleman Johnny" Burgoyne in two engagements, forcing his surrender and changing the tide of the revolution to favor the Americans.

Saratoga Battle history is the feature of the south loop trip. Fort Ticonderoga, immortalized in American history when Ethan Allen and his "Green Mountain Boys" took on the British regulars stationed there, is at the uppermost tip of the north loop. To really enjoy all this plus the superb scenery you should plan two days for each of these loops in upstate New York. Both tours start in Glens Falls.

Saratoga Springs is the first stop on the south loop. Famed for mineral springs this "Queen of the Spas" of the American Victorian era is famous also for Saratoga Racetrack and the National Museum of Thoroughbred Racing. It is also the home of a couple of strictly American habits—pie a la mode and Saratoga chips, the original potato chips.

You'll find some good flat cycling until you reach a long two mile climb into the Saratoga National Historical Park. Eight miles of paved road in the park take you to points of interest regarding the battle, as well as a monument to Benedict Arnold's leg.

The north loop traces along beside the Champlain Canal. Many pleasure boats and barges will drift by as you cycle along this flat area. If you get a chance, watch a boat pass through one of the several locks in operation on the canal.

The route continues north to Whitehall, known as the birthplace of the American Navy. The Naval Museum contains many artifacts and exhibits pertaining to early maritime history.

Between Whitehall and Ticonderoga the area develops into big rolling hills, but pedalable. You will find very few

Approx. mileage: South loop via Mechanicville, 70; north loop via Ticonderoga, 100.

Best times for touring: Memorial Day through Halloween.

Terrain: Flat stretches with intermittent hills, few steep grades.

Traffic: Moderate, with heavily traveled spots at tourist areas.

Historical points of interest: Saratoga National Historical Monument, Fort Ticonderoga, Fort William Henry.

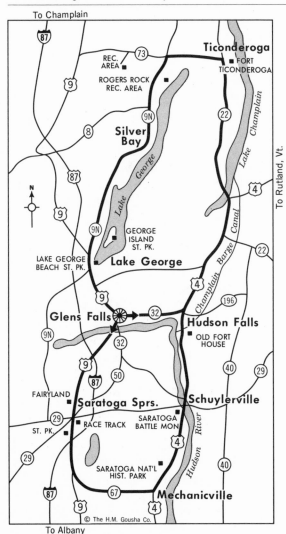

soft drink stops along here as there are no towns until Ticonderoga.

Lake Champlain is the beautiful site of the fort where Allen and his boys embarrassed the British "in the name of Great Jehovah and the Continental Congress." The fort has been restored and the museum contains Revolutionary War uniforms, sidearms and battle plans.

Riding south on State 9N takes you along scenic Lake George and past camping places. This road is fairly busy and has one tough four-mile stretch near Tongue Mountain. In the town of Lake George be sure to visit Fort William Henry, famous also in the Indian wars.

Lake George is excellent for swimming. Many motels and some guest houses are available on both loops, especially around Lake George, Saratoga Springs, and Fort Ticonderoga.

Circle of History from Bear Mountain

Such notables as George Washington and the Marquis de Lafayette are blended on this tour with Arlo Guthrie, Country Joe and the Fish, and the throngs of latter day, long-haired folks of Woodstock.

The tour begins at Bear Mountain Inn off U.S. 9. From here cross Bear Mountain Bridge to State Route 9D. About two miles up the road is Boscobel, an outstanding old restored home. Continue on 9D to the cutoff for Mt. Beacon and take a ride to the top for a breathtaking view of the Hudson Valley.

(An alternate trip through Brinkerhoff cuts off at the town of Beacon. Both Lafayette and Washington headquartered at the John Brinkerhoff house.)

Out of Beacon on the main route, follow 9D through Wappingers Falls where the road changes to U.S. 9. Pass through Poughkeepsie to Hyde Park, the home of Franklin Delano Roosevelt.

The house and library which contains photographs, papers and other memorabilia from FDR's life are on exhibit.

Further up U.S. 9 is the Vanderbilt Mansion Historical Site. This 700 acre estate has a 50-room house designed by Stanford White in 1895 for Frederick Vanderbilt.

If sight seeing has done you in, pull in to Norrie State Park where there are camping facilities and a restaurant. Next morning you will be fresh for a trek through the world's largest collection of individually owned antique airplanes. At the Old Rhinebeck Aerodrome you'll find a complete replica of a World War I airfield.

Near the Aerodrome bear left on Old Post Road, then left on Mt. Resten Road to State 199. Ride the Kingston-Rhinecliff Bridge to State 32 and south to State 9/W. Follow Flatbush Ave. and Albany Ave. into Kingston, the first capital of New York State. Visit the Old Senate House (1776) and the Old Dutch

Approximate mileage: 134; optional Woodstock trip, 30.

Best times for touring: Summer and fall.

Terrain: Paved roads. Hills, but not many really steep grades.

Traffic: Light or moderate except on main highways.

Historical points of interest: Brinkerhoff house, Roosevelt's Hyde Park, Vanderbilt mansion, Rhinebeck Aerodrome, old buildings in Kingston, Hurley, New Paltz; Woodstock; Newburgh.

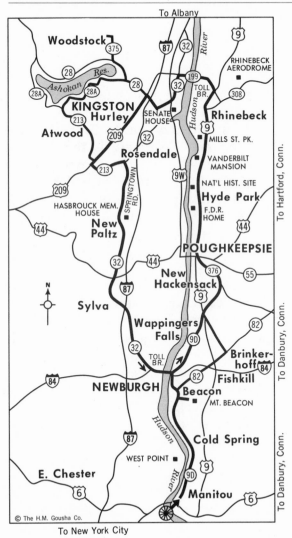

Church. Nearby Hurley is a 300-year old village.

Sidestep into a bit of modern history. The land of a thousand songs, dances and romances, the now legendary Woodstock was the happening place for the largest gathering of people the world has ever seen. There are motels available in this artists colony.

Ashokan Reservoir is circled to pick up the main route south to New Paltz. Founded in 1678 by Huguenots, the New Paltz stone houses, built mainly by the merchant families, are interesting Flemish architecture.

Pick up State 32 to Newburgh where you can visit another headquarters of George Washington. The Hasbrouck house is located high on a spectacular bluff over the river and is the subject of several well known paintings.

Take the bridge back across the Hudson and retrace your path to the Bear Mountain Inn.

Colonial Loop Around Both Sides of the Hudson

The famous landscapes of the Hudson River artists will come to life as you ride through some of the areas made familiar by their paintings in the late 1800's.

The Hudson River Valley has a colorful past. Henry Hudson, an Englishman sailing under the Dutch flag, cruised up the harbor in 1609. Henry didn't just float around the harbor but sailed almost as far north as present-day Albany. He liked what he saw and scooted back home to tell the folks. Soon Dutch colonists were settling all the way from the harbor to Albany. About this time, back in England, it occurred to somebody that John Cabot had explored this area in 1497 and naturally this meant England had prior claims to the territory. So off sailed the British and when they hit the New World they snatched up New York City. But peace prevailed and the Dutch went on living up the river.

The tour starts in Central Park. Follow the route out of the park stopping at such notable places as the Museum of Natural History and Grants Tomb.

Take Riverside Dr. to Broadway out to Yonkers. Near here is the Philipse Mansion. During the Revolutionary War the house was occupied by both the Americans and the British. In 1780, 16,000 British regulars encamped on the estate for several weeks; in 1871 the grounds were taken over by Colonial forces.

Look across the River to the famous Palisades. Continue on U.S. 9 through Dobbs Ferry, Tarrytown and into Ossing (Also, see page 42 for Sleepy Hollow and other points of interest.) Cut off to Quaker Bridge Road to avoid the U.S. 9 crossing on the Croton River.

From Peekskill the path to Bear Mountain Highway is a little difficult: Go north on Division to three streets north of Main, bear left on Highland Ave. to a left on U.S. 9. Continue past the junction of U.S. 202. Go west on U.S. 6-202 to Bear Mountain Bridge.

Approximate mileage: 100; Seven Lakes loop, 15.

Best times for touring: Summer or early fall.

Terrain: All roads paved but city streets are bumpy; some narrow throughways.

Traffic: Traffic is especially heavy on weekends.

Historical points of interest: Philipse Manor State Historical Site, Sleepy Hollow, Stony Point Battlefield.

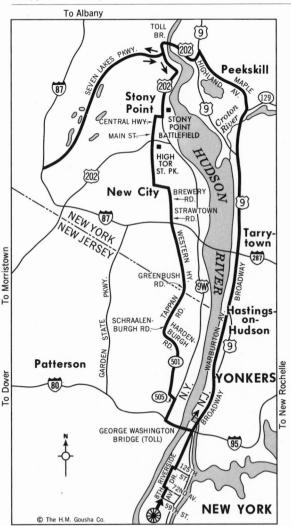

On the other side of the Hudson head south on U.S. 202-9W to the Bear Mountain Inn. Good grub here; you might want to hop off the bike and dig into a hearty lunch.

A 10-mile side trip into Bear Mountain State Park splits off the main route here. Follow Seven Lakes Parkway the entire route. There is a one-half mile stretch where a large junction will force you to walk your bike.

Back on the main route ride out to Stony Point, part of Gen. Washington's fortifications of the lower Hudson. Follow the map back to the George Washington Bridge. Use the sidewalk on the south side of the bridge. Exit on Broadway and retrace your route back to Central Park. (See page 44 for the Manhattan tour.)

Ride the Literary Route from Yonkers

America's literary heritage has deep roots in the area north of Yonkers and along the Hudson River. The homes of Thomas Paine, James Fenimore Cooper, and Washington Irving line this bike tour.

This is an easy riding, one day cruise, best toured on Sundays because there is less traffic. Clincher tires are recommended because of the debris.

Philipse Manor in Yonkers (Warburton and Dock St.) is a Georgian classic that both the English and the Revolutionists occupied. In 1682 Frederick Philipse was granted huge land holdings and became lord of the domain. His great-grandson, last lord of the Manor, was a Tory during the Revolution and found the Manor eventually snatched from him.

Out of Yonkers, at the Bronx River Parkway enter Mt. Vernon Ave. At the third light go left on Lincoln Ave. Turn left on North Ave. to the Thomas Paine cottage. This is the home of the famous pamphleteer of the *Common Sense Papers* during the Revolution.

Follow the map to the Mamaroneck Road site of the home of James Fenimore Cooper, author of *Last of the Mohicans*, one of America's first classics.

After crossing through White Plains, bear left on Virginia Rd. to Gen. Washington's headquarters during 1776. Demonstrations of colonial crafts are given in the Elijah Miller house where Washington planned strategy.

Crossing over toward the Hudson River, you enter Tarrytown and Sleepy Hollow country, made famous by Washington Irving. You won't see the Headless Horseman but you can visit Irving's home Sunnyside, south just off U.S. 9. The design is unusual, it is furnished with period antiques, and you can picnic on the grounds.

A little north of Tarrytown is the Philipsburg Manor, which marks the top boundary of the holdings of land

Approximate mileage: 40.

Best times for touring: Sundays during spring, summer, fall.

Terrain: All roads paved. Watch for roadside debris.

Traffic: Heavy, but roads are wide enough for safe cycling.

Historical points of interest: Philipse Manor Hall, Thomas Paine cottage, James Fenimore Cooper house, Washington's headquarters, Washington Irving's Sunnyside, Lyndhurst.

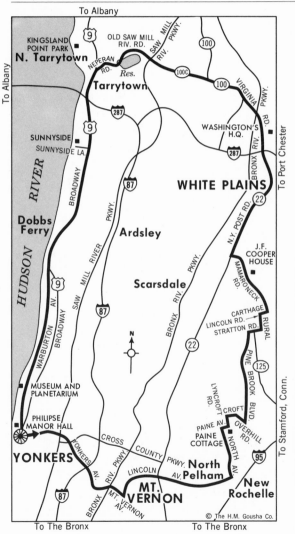

baron Philipse. The gristmill and two-story stone house were the hub of trading complex on the estate. Funds for restoration were provided by John D. Rockefeller, Jr.

South of Tarrytown is another imposing mansion. Lyndhurst was built by Jay Gould, who engineered notorious financial deals in the last decades of the 19th Century.

Also, see the tour on page 40 for other information on this strip of the Hudson.

Try a Sunday Ride on Manhattan Island

There is a lot to see in New York and this 20 mile tour weaves through many of the famous spots, but one must be prepared for cycling New York style.

First and most basic is the lock. Get a good one and use it every time you get off your bike. Next, worry about the traffic. A few rules to make your trip safe: Stay in the curb lane, motorists expect you to be there. Ride slowly, especially in heavy traffic. Get a horn or some type of loud noise maker and don't be afraid to beep. A mirror is also useful when weaving through the cars. A sometimes very dangerous New York cycling problem is potholes. If you see a pothole and it's too late to avoid it (never try to dodge one in heavy traffic), slow down and pedal straight over it. If you try to angle you may flip the bike.

O.K., you're ready to ride. Try a Sunday—there is less traffic. Start at W. 125th St., stopping soon for a look at Grant's Tomb. Pass Columbia University and head into Central Park on 72nd St. This is beautiful riding area. Horses, trees, all types of shrubbery, along with the "park people," lovers, nannies and rich little folks, park strollers and other bike riders all congregate here.

Some great museums are in the Park. The American Museum of Natural History houses millions of zoological, geographical, anthropological and botanical specimens from all over the globe. The jewel collection gained worldwide notoriety when three Florida beach boys, inspired by a Hollywood movie, pulled off the most daring jewel theft in recent history. The hardy boys cut their way through a transom on the fourth floor and made off with the 553 carat Star of India, among other gems. Most of the jewels were recovered.

The Metropolitan Museum of Art houses one of the most comprehensive collections in the world. Inside the imposing old building are more than a

Approximate mileage: 20.

Best times for touring: Any time when weather permits. Sundays are best.

Terrain: Bikeways and city streets.

Traffic: You're in New York, need we say more?

Historical points of interest: Grant's Tomb, Museum of Natural History, Lincoln Center, Metropolitan Museum of Art.

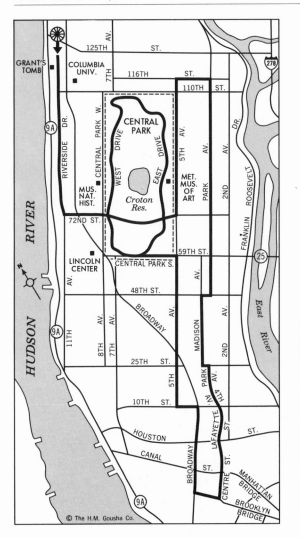

million art treasures representing the work of 50 centuries.

Just outside the Park is the Lincoln Center for the Performing Arts. This cultural and educational complex includes Philharmonic Hall and the Metropolitan Opera House. Have lunch in an artistic atmosphere at one of the cafes along here.

South of the Park follow the map to Fifth Ave.; marvel at the shops and watch out for the traffic. Past Rockefeller Center, continue down Fifth Ave. to fabled Broadway, almost to the tip of Manhattan Island. The loop back along Park Ave., crosses Central Park back to the departure point.

New York 45

A Cycling Charge Up Sagamore Hill

From a Merchant Marine Academy to the home of rough ridin' Teddy Roosevelt this 50-mile tour through the Oyster Bay area offers the cyclist a variety of New York sights.

The trip has all hard surfaced roads but some are bumpy. Because of traffic conditions, Sunday is preferred for touring. Especially in the estate area around Old Westbury Rd. some roads are narrow, and you will encounter a few hills in the north shore terrain.

The tour begins at the U.S. Merchant Marine Academy at Kings Point, accessible by taking State Route 25A to 11A and following the signs to the Academy. One of five U.S. military service schools, the Academy is open on weekends and welcomes visitors to the Regimental Review on Saturdays at 10:30 a.m.

Leave Kings Point via Steamboat Rd. to Middle Neck Rd. and Hicks Lane, then to East Shore Rd. that traces Manhasset Bay. Follow the map to the spot where State 101 ends and continue south on Searingtown Rd. up the hill. Ride left at Diana's Trail, then right after Morley Park onto The Tulips. Elm St. then takes you to Mineola Av. and along the route to Oyster Bay.

Raynham Hall is a colonial house just at Oyster Bay. The Hall, circa 1740, was the Revolutionary War headquarters of British Lt. Col. John Graves Simcoe and his Queen's Rangers. It was also the family home of Robert Townsend, George Washington's main secret agent for the Long Island area.

This area has become synonymous with the name of the man who "carried a big stick". The grave of Theodore Roosevelt is on Main Street and a short haul up Cove Neck Rd. leads to Sagamore Hill, his estate. It contains such "T. R." paraphernalia as elephant tusks from the Emperor of Ethiopia, rugs from the Sultan of Turkey and the pistol Roosevelt used on his charge up San Juan Hill.

Approximate mileage: 52.

Best times for touring: Winter is usually too cold.

Terrain: All roads paved, some bumpy; mostly flat with gently rolling hills.

Traffic: Generally not too heavy except at major crossroads.

Historical points of interest: Raynham Hall, Grave of Theodore Roosevelt, Sagamore Hill.

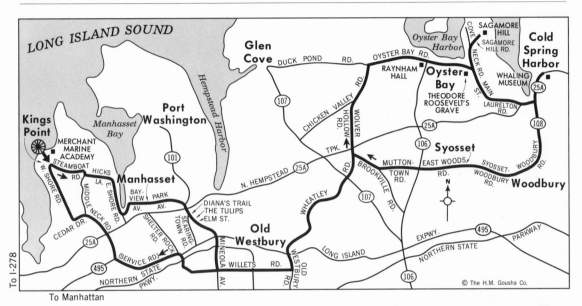

To I-278

To Manhattan

Return to Main Street and go left to Laurelton Rd. and left again at State Route 25A. Follow the signs out to Cold Spring Harbor and the Whaling Museum. Open from May to November, the museum has a fine collection of relics from the whaling days when Cold Spring Harbor was one of New York's main ports of the last century.

Follow the route through Syosset back to the service road adjacent to State 495 and on into Kings Point.

Easy Excursion to Erie's Naval History

A ship, a monument and an elephant are all part of this tour through the city of Erie, Pennsylvania.

The ride begins at Zuck Park (accessible off Interstate 79). Take Zuck Road to 26th St. and head up Peninsula Drive (State 832). Continue along the route past the Waldameer Amusement Park. From here you will cycle down across 3,100 acres of beautiful, lush playground around Presque Isle Bay. There's water skiing, swimming and, if you're a hearty soul out during the winter, ice fishing.

Follow the Peninsula Roadway around to the Perry Monument, a tall structure commemorating Commodore Oliver Hazard Perry's battle of Lake Erie in 1813. The fearless Perry floated his ships across sandbars to fight the British and deliver his famous line "Don't give up the ship."

Take the Roadway back to West 6th St. and go left. The *U.S.S. Niagara* is at the foot of State St. The boat is the restored hull of Perry's boat which sunk in Misery Bay.

Further down the street is the Anthony Wayne Blockhouse, a replica of the blockhouse where General "Mad Anthony" Wayne died in 1796 after becoming ill on a voyage. He was buried here at the foot of the flagpole, but his remains were moved later by his son.

Just past the blockhouse go right on East Ave. to 26th St. and head right to Glenwood Park Ave., past Erie Stadium. The end of the tour is the Glenwood Park Zoo, and the elephant we promised.

Approximate mileage: 36.

Best times for touring: Early spring or fall.

Terrain: City streets, tree-clad parkway.

Traffic: Generally light except for rush hours.

Historical points of interest: *U.S.S. Niagara,* Anthony Wayne Blockhouse, Admiral Perry Monument.

"Black Gold" Tour to World's First Oil Well

The lust for "black gold" had its beginnings on this Pennsylvania tour. A replica of the world's first oil well at the original site is the highlight of this Keystone State excursion.

At Fort Le Boeuf on U.S. 19 in Waterford is the former site of three different forts; one French, one British and finally an American garrison to protect settlers. The Judson House, built in 1820, now stands on the site to commemorate George Washington's first public mission. A statue shows Washington giving a notice from the governor of Virginia to the French, saying they were trespassing on British soil.

The tour takes State 97 out of Waterford to Union City. Once an agriculture town, Union City was diverted to oil when the refineries began opening as early as 1862.

From here you follow State 8 through Tillotson to Titusville. Overnight, Titusville became, after Edwin L. Drake completed the first successful oil well, the oil capital of the country.

Oil had been prevalent along Oil Creek, near the area, for some time. But nobody knew what to do with it until Samuel Kier produced a successful illuminant by distilling the petroleum. The previously used whale oil was becoming too costly, so the discovery led to more experiments and finally a cry for "oil."

Drake showed up at Oil Creek and ran into a bit of a problem; he didn't know how to get the stuff out of the ground. He tried to excavate but just made a mess. In 1859 he came back and, with the assistance of "Uncle Billy" Smith, a blacksmith, he devised a drill using a method learned from salt wells.

On Sunday afternoon, August 28, 1859, Uncle Billy sauntered out to their "well" and saw the precious black goo floating just a few feet below the derrick floor. What happened next has become an auto maker's delight and a conservationist's nightmare; the country

Approx. mileage: Waterford-Titusville round trip, 60; Pithole loop, 22; Allegheny loop, 25.

Best times for touring: Any season except winter.

Terrain: Rolling countryside.

Traffic: No problem.

Historical points of interest: Drake Well, Fort Le Boeuf, Pithole Ghost Town.

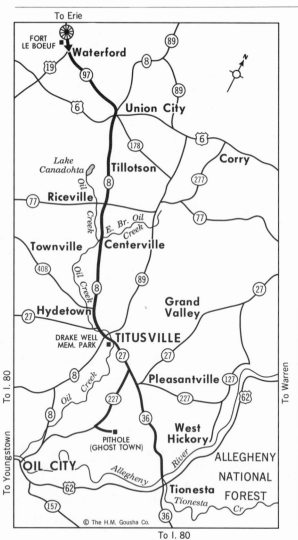

went wild and wells sprang up everywhere.

Today on the location is an operating replica of Drake's derrick along with a museum depicting the history of the event. Open daily. Admission 50 cents.

An interesting side trip lies south on State Routes 27 and 227, along the Road known as the Pennsylvania Trail of History. Ten miles down the road is Pithole city, a ghost town on a hillside where once 10,000 oil hunters tried to make their fortunes. Another extra excursion is down State Route 36 to the Allegheny National Forest.

Philadelphia–the City of "Firsts"

Despite W. C. Fields' jabs at this famous colonial city, Philadelphia is hardly dull; offering the cyclist a lot of history for the mileage. Plan a leisurely pace to allow the "Cradle of the Nation" to unveil its rich heritage.

Philadelphia is a city of "firsts", including the first American hospital, bank, daily newspaper and U.S. Mint. But it is most noted for its role as the "first city" of the Revolution. Both Continental Congresses convened here and "Philly" became the headquarters for the War for Independence.

The tour which leads through the core of the hotbed of the Revolution begins at Marconi Plaza. From here take Moyamensing Ave. out to Fifth St. and turn left. Continue up the street to Independence National Historical Park and Independence Mall State Park.

The historical sights are clustered here in about a five block square and are too numerous to mention. A partial listing and brief description include: Independence Hall (1732), the site of the signing of the Declaration of Independence and home of the Liberty Bell; Congress Hall, meeting place for the U.S. Congress during the last decade of the 18th century; First Bank of the United States (1795); Christ Church, where Washington and members of the Continental Congress worshipped. There is the Betsy Ross House with memorabilia and household items from the home of the seamstress who is said to have made the American Flag; Franklin's grave; First U.S. Mint, Free Quaker Meeting House, Atwater Kent Museum, with hundreds of exhibits of city's early history, scenes of Indian and Colonial days.

The tour continues along Fifth which veers left, becoming Germantown Ave. Near here in the Battle of Germantown on October 3, 1777, Washington was defeated by British forces. Follow Germantown Ave. to Lehigh Ave. and

Approximate mileage: 20.

Best times for touring: Any season, bundle up in the winter.

Terrain: City streets.

Traffic: Can be rough, be especially careful leaving Fairmount Park.

Historical points of interest: Independence Hall, Betsy Ross House, Franklin's grave, First Quaker Meeting House, Franklin Institute Museum and Planetarium, City Hall.

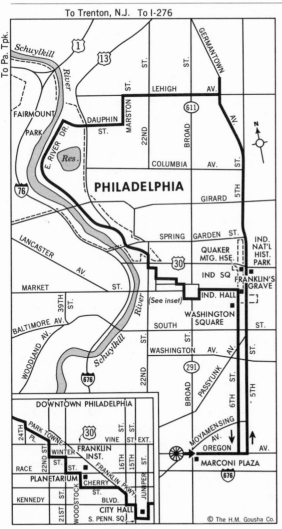

turn left. At Marston Street make another left to Dauphin and head out to Fairmount Park via East River Drive. The route will parallel the Schuylkill River through the park as it passes some interesting mansions. Be careful leaving the park as the traffic can be hazardous.

Take Park Towne to 22nd Street and follow the map until you reach the Rodin Museum (largest collection of Rodin's works outside of Paris). There pick up 21st to the Franklin Institute Museum and Planetarium. The buildings house exhibits on all facets of space exploration and various other sciences.

Follow the route around City Hall and back to Sixth St. Oregon Ave. will lead you back to the departure point.

Hilly Ride on the French-Indian War Trail

An ancient tollhouse greets the cyclist as he pedals along the Pennsylvania trail of history past points important in the French and Indian Wars. The route is a hilly one and is recommended for the strong rider.

The tour begins in Farmington off U.S. 40. Just outside of the town is Fort Necessity National Battlefield.

It was here that George Washington rose to prominence in the conflict that opened the French and Indian War. Washington, then a lieutenant, marched westward with an army of Virginians in April 1754, to contest French possession of the forks of the Ohio River. Washington and his forces drove a small band of French from the area. Fort Necessity was then built as a temporary defensive work. On July 3, the French returned with a much larger force and forced the Virginians to surrender. At the battlefield is a stockade, storehouse and entrenchments, all reconstructed on their original locations.

General Edward Braddock's grave is nearby. He died in 1775 as he led his British troops against the French, hoping to drive the French from the Upper Ohio Valley. There is a monument and plaque at the site.

The tour continues on U.S. 40 to Uniontown. (There is an optional route from here to Connellsville. Avoid U.S. 119 because of traffic. Take the road through Bute and pick up State 201 in Connellsville.)

Just past Uniontown is the Searights Tollhouse. Don't reach for money, the house no longer collects tolls but stands as a reminder of the days when the flow of traffic was so steady that this "National Road" was a gate to the West.

The route follows U.S. 40 to a 1790's trading post, Bowman's Castle, then heads east to State Route 201. Turn right on State 31 and continue past West Newton. A few miles further watch the signs for a road heading north to Herminie. Take this road to State

Approx. mileage: 55 miles via Brownsville, 65 via Connellsville.

Best times for touring: Spring, fall or summer.

Terrain: Very hilly, a safe flag and strong legs are recommended.

Traffic: Light.

Historical points of interest: Bushy Run Battlefield, Braddock's Grave, Fort Necessity, Searights Tollhouse.

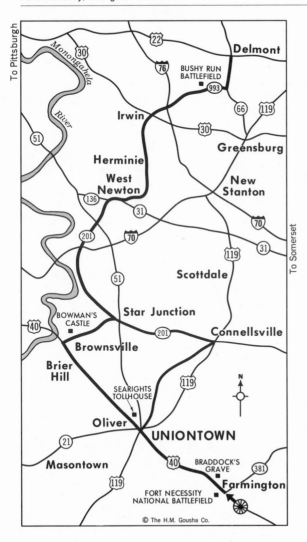

Route 993 and Bushy Run Battlefield.

A major British victory against the most serious Indian threat to the colonial frontier was accomplished at Bushy Run. Called Pontiac's "rebellion," for the chief who engineered the uprising, it almost threw the white man back to the Atlantic. The Indians began in 1763 and before they were through they had captured every fort along a thousand mile frontier, except Forts Niagara, Detroit and Pitt.

Colonel Henry Bouquet was dispatched to bring supplies to the starving troops at Fort Pitt. In August of 1763, Bouquet's army was surrounded and attacked by 1,500 Indians. His forces totaled 500. Bouquet rounded up his men and used the supplies as a barricade. He then pulled off a daring bluff; he faked a withdrawal of his advance guard. The trick worked, the Indians came out of the woods and this opening led the British to a total victory.

Good stopping places for food are at West Newton, Manor, and Brier Hill.

Valley Forge and Washington's Crossing

This 120-mile tour can aptly be described as a ride through "George Washington country," as some of his most famous feats took place here in the southeastern part of Pennsylvania.

Mechanics Grove on U.S. 222 is a good starting place because a short distance south you can visit the birthplace of Robert Fulton, artist, engineer, gun designer and inventor. A few miles later leave much of the traffic and turn onto State 272. Ride through the countryside on State 10, turning right on State 926. Follow it to the intersection of State 841.

Here you can opt for the Battle of Brandywine side trip that is highly recommended for historical interest (but the traffic is heavy).

The Battle of Brandywine on September 11, 1777, was the only major clash of the two main armies during the campaign that ended in the British capture of Philadelphia. George Washington led a force of about 11,000 against British and Hessian troops numbering near 18,000. Although defeated, Washington and his men came out of the battle with the majority intact.

On this optional ride also is Chadds Ford, homegrounds of the famous American family of artists, the Wyeths.

Back on the main route continue along State Route 842 past West Chester, past Chatwood, Malvern and up to Phoenixville. The tour now takes State Route 23 to Valley Forge, located high above the Schuylkill River.

First settled by workers at an iron forge begun in 1742, the fort and part of the village were burned by the British in 1777. The area is most noted as Washington's quarters during the horrible winter of 1777–78 when the elements, lack of supplies, failure of Congress to provide money and losses to the British had the unpaid, volunteer army's morale at its lowest state. Reconstructions of this camp can be visited.

Leaving Valley Forge, cross the

Approximate mileage: 120; 15 additional for Brandywine tour.

Best times for tourings: May is superb—the dogwood is in bloom; summer is often too hot, winter too cold.

Terrain: Fair roads, rolling hills.

Traffic: Generally light, can be heavy on Brandywine road.

Historical points of interest: Robert Fulton's birthplace, Valley Forge, Mercer Museum, Brandywine Battlefield, Washington's Delaware Crossing.

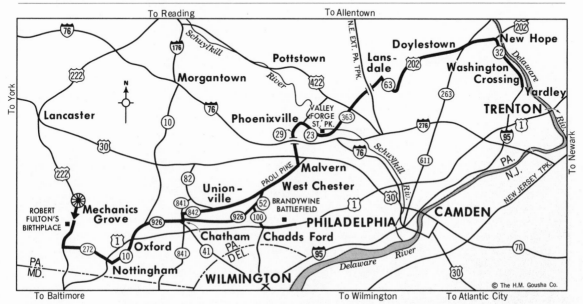

Schuylkill and ride State 363 up to State 63. Pick up U.S. 202 to Doyles-town. Here the bright red tile roofed Mercer Museum contains a collection of approximately 25,000 implements, utensils and machines used in this country before 1820.

When you reach the Delaware River turn right on State 32 and parallel the river to the site of Washington's brilliant military maneuver that helped turn the tide of the Revolution.

On Christmas night, 1776, he had the main American force ferried across the Delaware. In the early morning hours his men made the march to Trenton. The Hessian garrison was taken completely by surprise.

A state park houses memorabilia from the crossing. On the riverbank is the Old Ferry Inn, with an ell of the original structure. Also, Emanuel Leutze's famous painting "Washington Crossing the Delaware" is displayed.

Mid-Atlantic

Easy Victorian Beach Cruise Along Cape May

Victorian houses, places important in history, wildlife sanctuaries and the best of the New Jersey beaches are the treats on this 45-mile ride. Many of the roads are lightly traveled, with safe, wide shoulders. The summer breezes are light in the morning with velocity increasing toward afternoon.

Cape May City has an early American air displayed in the Colonial architecture of some of the homes. Residents claim that Cape May has more descendants of the Mayflower pilgrims than any other county.

Take time to explore the city. The old country store in Cape May Courthouse is a charming step into the past. Many Victorian homes line a three mile bike route mapped by the Cape May County Planning Board, available at the Courthouse.

At the airport, an airline executive has set up a unique museum of transportation in one of the hangars, featuring historic vehicles from all over the world, including a locomotive and a San Francisco cable car.

The tour heads north passing through the Wildwood resorts, a favorite of families, with its long stretches of beach and gentle surf.

Up the road at Stone Harbor large groups of people and birds flock to watch each other. Over 5,000 tropical birds summer here in nesting grounds at 111th Street in the city.

Ocean City, further north on the route, is a place of mansions and leisure. Victorian structures abound. And, with the sails from boats fluttering in the breeze as a backdrop to a lobster dinner, you may find it hard to get back on your bike.

The three Lake brothers, all Methodist ministers, founded the area back in 1879 and decreed that the religious resort should be sans liquor and it remains so today. A son of one of the Lake brothers, Simon Lake, dabbled in submarines and eventually sold

Approximate mileage: 45.

Best times for touring: Spring and summer,

Terrain: Relatively flat along the coast.

Traffic: Can be rough on weekends and holidays.

Historical points of interest: Cape May houses, Courthouse; Ocean City Historical Museum, Somers House.

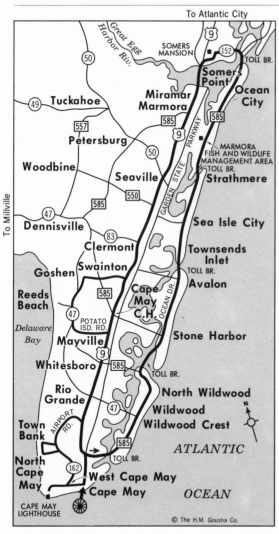

seven of his three-wheeled underwater machines to the Russians after being turned down by the U.S. Navy. He is also credited with inventing the periscope.

At the Ocean City Historical Museum exhibits from the ship *Sindia* are displayed. It seems the vessel loaded with Christmas goodies was stranded on a nearby beach and locals went on a large scale scavenger hunt.

The next stop is Somers Mansion, the home built in 1720 by the great-grandfather of one of America's naval heroes. In 1804, Richard Somers and twelve volunteers made his ketch into a floating mine to blow up pirate ships. The escape plan failed and the crew was killed. Now a historic site, the house contains family antiques.

From here follow U.S. 9 back to the departure point at Cape May, ending your coastal cruise. An optional loop is indicated on the map.

Bicycle Closeup of Washington, D.C.

The historic splendor of our nation's Capital is unveiled for the cyclist on this 25-mile loop tour through the streets of Washington, D.C. On a bike you can take your time and see the famous sights close up. Also, you can utilize bike paths.

The tour begins at the Capitol building, between Constitution and Independence Aves. The building has been enlarged many times since Washington laid the cornerstone in 1793. It was completely rebuilt after the British burned it in 1814.

Riding up Third, go adjacent to Madison Dr., then cross the street on Fourth. On Sixth St. is the National Gallery of Art, which contains western art from the 12th to 20th centuries, including the only Leonardo da Vinci painting in America.

The route now makes a big loop passing the Corcoran Gallery of Art on the left. The gallery has an outstanding collection of 18th-20th century American art.

You now pass 1600 Pennsylvania Ave., the home of every president since John Adams—the White House. Burned by the British in the War of 1812, the three-story building has been remodeled many times. After sightseeing, loop over 17th and cross back over Constitution Ave. to circle the Washington Monument.

A 555-foot obelisk, the monument, finished in 1884, offers an outstanding view from windows at the 500-foot level. You can walk up 898 steps or take the elevator for 10 cents. Open daily.

From here the tour edges the great Reflecting Pool to the Lincoln Memorial and continues along the Potomac with an alternate tour around West Basin Drive. The famous cherry trees line the Tidal Basin.

The main tour now heads north past the Jefferson Monument and returns to Independence Ave.

Approximate mileage: 25.

Best times for touring: Mid-spring for the cherry blossoms; fall.

Terrain: Bikeways and city streets.

Traffic: Avoid rush hours. Be wary of open car doors, sudden stops, turns.

Historical points of interest: Capitol, Corcoran Gallery of Art, Jefferson Memorial, Lincoln Memorial, National Gallery of Art, Smithsonian Institute, Washington Monument, White House.

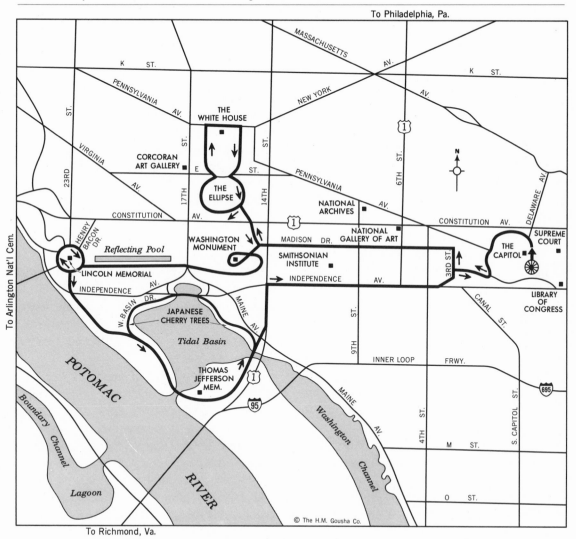

Arlington-Alexandria Ride on the Potomac

Washington, D.C. and the immediate area has an abundance of historical sights. Keep alert to traffic and it should add up to a pleasant 25-mile ride.

The tour begins at the Lincoln Memorial, which can be reached via 23rd St. or U.S. 50.

The Lincoln Memorial has been described with every adjective conceivable, but the one word that stands out is *inspiring*. The view from the monument is magnificent, the fabled Potomac River on one side, and on the other a view across the Reflecting Pool and the Mall to the Washington Monument.

Cyclists should cross the Arlington Memorial Bridge riding on the right sidewalk and making use of sidewalks all the way to the entrance of Arlington Cemetery.

Among the many men who served their country and have been buried at Arlington, our nation's largest national cemetery, are Presidents William Howard Taft and John F. Kennedy. No automobiles are allowed, but the right smile may get your bike past a guard. If not, have a good lock ready and leave your cycle locked at the main gate.

After leaving Arlington, again stay to the right sidewalk and walk your bike across the roads. You will easily get on Lady Bird Bike Path. The route follows the Potomac and you will soon see the Pentagon Building across the Lagoon to your right. (Your chance to shorten the tour comes at George Mason Memorial Bridge. Follow route back to Lincoln Memorial). Pass Washington National Airport and later ride parallel to a mass of railroad tracks.

Cycle down Pitt Street to King St., where you turn right for Alexandria. In 1732 a group of Scotch merchants established a tobacco warehouse at the junction of Hunting Creek and the "Potowmack" River. The settlement prospered and 17 years later "John West, Mr., surveyor," and his young assistant, George Washington, arrived

Approximate mileage: 25, one way to Alexandria.

Best time for touring: Spring or fall; winter can be enjoyable if you dress warmly.

Terrain: Sidewalks, bikeways, and city streets that demand caution.

Traffic: O.K. if cyclist keeps alert for certain hazards — open car doors, sudden stops or turns by motorists, and rush hours.

Historical points of interest: Lincoln Memorial, Arlington National Cemetery, Washington Masonic National Memorial, Gadsby Tavern, Carlyle House.

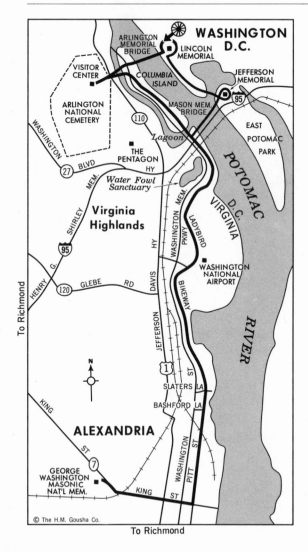

To Richmond

and "laid off in streets and 84 half-acre lots" the town of Alexandria.

Near the junction of State Route 7 and Pitt St. at 121 N. Fairfax is the home of one of the original Scottish merchants, John Carlyle. A museum since 1900, the house is replete with the original furnishings, graceful curved stairway, and a fireplace with blue marble facing. George Washington held a conference here which resulted in the Constitutional Convention.

The tour follows State 7 to the George Washington Masonic Memorial. On the way, one street to the right at 400 Cameron Street, is Gadsby's Tavern. Now an American Legion Post, it once was a famous hostelry, frequented by Washington.

The Masonic Memorial, the last stop on the tour, was patterned after the ancient lighthouse at Alexandria, Egypt. The 333-foot high building has an observation platform, organ and relics of Washington's term as Master of Alexandria-Washington Lodge of Masons.

Civil War Country – Harpers Ferry to Antietam

Harpers Ferry, where John Brown's party whooped down in an ill-fated raid, is the take-off point for this short tour that can easily take two days if you want to absorb all of the Civil War history it offers.

On the cliffs where Thomas Jefferson once journeyed to see a view "worth a voyage across the Atlantic," Harpers Ferry has been restored as a historic community. From here you ride the 35-mile round trip that takes you to Antietam, site of an intense Civil War battle in 1862.

(A good 10-speed bicycle with low gears is recommended because the Old Harpers Ferry Road has a number of tough, but scenic, hills. Normally, you would probably ride the old C & O Canal towpath to Antietam Aqueduct, but it was severely damaged in flooding and may be closed throughout 1973.)

Before you leave Harpers Ferry (or the AYH hostel at Sandy Hook, if you are staying there), ride to Stagecoach Inn, built in 1826, and pick up sightseeing information at the visitor center there. Among the town's preserved buildings is the enginehouse used as a fort by John Brown when the fiery abolitionist hit in an abortive raid in 1859.

An important arms producing center, the community was brought into prominence by the Civil War and into eventual decline until it was preserved as a historical park.

Work your way up a stiff hill past Harper House and the Marmion Row houses to Hilltop House, an excellent restaurant (crab cakes, baked ham and hot biscuits) where, from the broad porches, you can see three states and the junction of the Potomac and Shenandoah Rivers.

Cross the river and follow the route to Antietam Aqueduct on the Canal. There are campgrounds here if you are saving the battlefield tour for the next day.

Approx. mileage: 35 round trip from Harpers Ferry; 20 from Antietam.

Best times for touring: Spring and fall; winter bleak, summer hot.

Terrain: A few difficult hills. Ten-speeds recommended.

Traffic: Moderate.

Historical points of interest: Harpers Ferry National Historical Park, Antietam National Battlefield Site, C & O Canal.

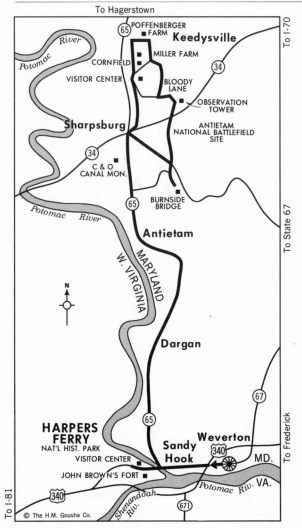

Ride through Sharpsburg, turning right briefly on State 34 and then left on State 65 to the visitor center at Antietam. They have detailed maps of a tour to follow over eight miles of paved roads tracing battlelines of one of the most desperate attacks of the war. At one spot, Bloody Lane, a point-blank confrontation claimed 4,000 dead in three hours, September 17, 1862.

The battle at Antietam was a decisive one, marking General Lee's failure to push the war into the north. England postponed help to the Confederates, and President Lincoln issued his Emancipation Proclamation five days after the Federal victory.

After your tour retrace your route either to the Canal or back to Harpers Ferry.

Scenic Rural Route on the Eastern Shore

A few dozen miles on the quiet Eastern Shore give you large doses of the way of life that has continued in Maryland for three centuries. This section has no big towns. Instead there are rural villages connected with sandy shorelines that haven't changed at all.

Spring and fall are the best times to ride; expect some strong winds in the fall. Summers can be hot, winters cold and windy. This is a nice, easy ride and 3-speed bikes are ok. You will be bothered more with traffic on Sunday than other days, but there are very good shoulders along most of the route. Drive to Easton and unload your bikes somewhere near U.S. 50. Cruise past the old town's elegantly restored Colonial homes and the old Tidewater Inn. On the outskirts of town pick up State 333 for a scenic rural route to Oxford.

Second only to Annapolis as one of Maryland's earliest settlements, Oxford has always depended on the Bay. Once a port of entry for tobacco and ships supplies, it is still important in boat building and fishing.

The good food at Robert Morris Inn makes it an ideal stopping place for lunch. A bonus is the 18th century home itself. After lunch you may want to visit shipyards before boarding the ferry that will carry you across the Tred Avon River. It will cost a mere 25 cents to use the oldest working ferry boat in the United States. On Sundays it rests.

It is only a short sprint to Royal Oak where Pasadena Conference is located. This quaint old estate, complete with swimming pool and German chef, is a good stopping place for a group ride and a meal.

Pass the turn onto State 329 and continue on State 33 to St. Michaels and an absorbing few hours at the Chesapeake Bay Maritime Museum. St. Michaels earned its early fame from the variety of watercrafts built in its yards—broad pungys, schooners, skipjacks and log canoes.

Approximate mileage: 35; loop trip—additional 30.

Best times for touring: Spring and fall; summers hot, winters windy.

Terrain: Level countryside. Good shoulders on most of route.

Traffic: Less on Saturday. Tred Avon Ferry does not run on Sunday.

Historical points of interest: Chesapeake Bay Maritime Museum, Tred Avon Ferry, the towns of Oxford and St. Michaels.

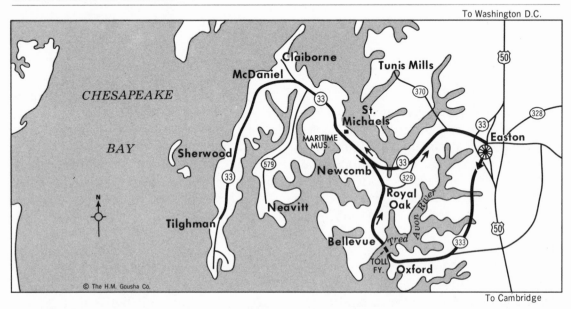

Leafy lanes lead to the broad street and harbor that are the Maritime Museum. Afloat are several ancient sailing vessels and facing the water is a string of beautifully restored houses. The museum is bent upon preserving the three and a half century-old way of life and crafts of the Bay in a collection of drawings, shipbuilding memorabilia, shipping records and, of course, the boats themselves as well as the old houses. Closed Monday. Admission. Need still more Chesapeake Bay scenery? Take the optional loop out to Tilghman and back. Or, have a meal at the Crab Claw before riding back to Easton.

Colonial Williamsburg and Jamestown Junket

If you are interested in American history plan to spend several days on this Virginia tour recycling America's past.

The tour starts in Williamsburg, accessible via U.S. 60. Campgrounds are available at Five Forks Tent and Trailer Camp, three miles west on State 5. This early settlement (1633) was restored by funds from John D. Rockefeller II. Formerly called Middle Plantation, the name was changed when the state house in Jamestown burned and Williamsburg became the capital of the Crown Colony of Virginia. The College of William and Mary, the second college in America, was founded here in 1633. Thomas Jefferson, George Washington and Patrick Henry were among the famous people that lived in the town.

The next stop on this historical jaunt is Jamestown, the first permanent, English speaking colony in America. Names such as John Smith, Pocahontas and John Rolfe are connected with the beginnings of the settlement. Across the James River by the ferry is Smith's Flat Plantation, given to John Rolfe by Powhatan, Pocahontas' father.

The route heads northeast to the Richmond National Battlefield Park. Stop here for a look before continuing on to Richmond, the capital city of the Confederacy. It held that distinction for four years until it was burned. Now the capital of Virginia, the city offers many historical highlights. Visit the Governor's Mansion built between 1811 and 1813, the Historic Museum at General Lee's home, the Confederate Museum, and the Virginia House. The Edgar Allen Poe Museum is located in what is believed the oldest standing building in Richmond. Camping facilities are available at Shady Hill Mobile park, two miles south. If you fancy some fine food you're in the right town, Richmond is noted for its southern cuisine.

The route becomes more hilly and beautiful as you approach the Blue

Approximate mileage: 175.

Best times for touring: Mid-September, October and early November, and May.

Terrain: Good paved roads, some hills before Charlottesville.

Traffic: Local traffic heavy near large towns.

Historical points of interest: Williamsburg, Jamestown, Richmond, Edgar Allen Poe Museum, homes of Madison, and Monroe, Monticello.

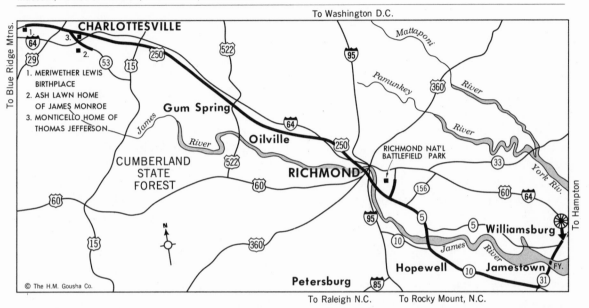

Ridge Mountains on your way to Charlottesville, the home of Thomas Jefferson, James Madison, and James Monroe.

Named for Queen Charlotte, wife of King George III, the city was founded in 1762 at the foothills of the Blue Ridge Mountains. Places to visit include Monticello, Jefferson's famous home which he designed, University of Virginia, also a Jefferson product. He planned, founded and designed the institute. Ash Lawn, James Monroe's estate was, you guessed it, also designed by Jefferson.

"Give me a beer or give me death" isn't quite the way it went, but it seems apropos when speaking of Mitchie Tavern, birthplace of famed orator and governor, Patrick Henry. Camping is available at Cambrae Lodge KOA eight miles south off U.S. 29.

Hatteras – Pirates and a Lost Colony

The ocean breezes whisper tales of pirates and lost colonies as you pedal along the string of barrier islands that curve a bony finger around North Carolina's shore.

The tour begins in Elizabeth City, an important Colonial trading port. The Winslow Home in the city is the site of Culpepper's Rebellion, the first open revolt against the King of England, in 1677.

Crossing over now to the Outer Banks, the skinny line of barrier islands, you will pass near Kitty Hawk and Kill Devil Hills. At the Wright Brothers Memorial you can see the landing strip of the first flight. The visitor center has a reproduction of the first airplane and the story of its invention.

At Nags Head take the turn to Manteo and Fort Raleigh. Manteo was the site of the historic Civil War battle of Roanoke Island where Gen. Burnsides won the fight and with it control of northeastern North Carolina for the Union.

Fort Raleigh was the first English colony in America. Established in 1585, the settlers were apparently flourishing when Governor John White left for England for supplies. He was detained by the war with Spain and didn't return until 1590. The only remains of the colony were the words CROATOAN cut into a tree. What the word means and what happened to the colony is still a mystery.

Virginia Dare, born August 18, 1587, in the colony was the first child of English parentage born in what is now the United States.

Back on the main route the tour heads south to Cape Hatteras National Seashore and to the town of Buxton. Near here is the Cape Hatteras Lighthouse, jutting up 208 feet to warn ships against the waters known as the "Graveyard of the Atlantic."

At Hatteras, a small sea village, with

Approximate mileage: 200.	
Best times for touring: Spring (avoid tourist season).	
Terrain: Absolutely flat over good paved roads.	
Traffic: Not bad during the spring months.	

Historical points of interest: Elizabeth City, Kitty Hawk, Manteo, Fort Raleigh National Historic Site, Cape Hatteras Lighthouse, Blackbeard's Hideout, Alphonso Whaling Museum, Tryon Palace Restoration.

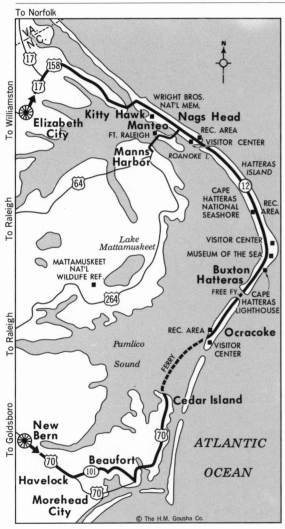

interesting local folk, you'll take the free ferry across the water and then pedal down to Ocracoke.

Ocracoke was the stomping grounds of Edward Teach, better known as the infamous pirate "Blackbeard". From "Teach's Hole", Blackbeard ran his pirate affairs, sharing booty with the governor of North Carolina. The pirate bit his last dubloon in this hideout; he was killed here by a Virginian, Lieutenant Maynard, in 1718.

Nearing the end of the jaunt is the sea coast town of Beaufort. Spots to see include; The Old Burying Ground (eerie tales are told about this place), Alphonso Whaling Museum and the Joseph Bell House built in 1767. The tour ends in New Bern but the sightseeing is better than ever. Visit the Christ Church, Federal Building, Firemen's Museum and Tryon Palace Restoration. There are campgrounds and motels all along the route, so you may conveniently divide the tour into several easy days riding.

Rugged "Dark Corner" Ride in the Carolinas

Two days in this rugged "Dark Corner" tour of South Carolina demand a low geared bike and strong leg muscles. But for the cyclist who decides to challenge the steep hills the scenic rewards are many—crystal streams and winding roads in provincial back country.

The best time to take this tour is in October when the steel-colored rocky cliffs are contrasted with the dazzling yellows, reds and orange of the mountain hardwoods. If fall is your time to head for the hills be sure to bring warm clothing; it gets cold at night. Another precaution advisable on this tour: bring your own tire repair essentials as there aren't any shops along the route.

The first day of the tour begins after breakfast at Table Rock State Park. Take the west gate road out of the campground to State 11 and proceed to the left. About two miles up the road make another left on Saluda Hill Baptist Church Road. Cross a small mountain ridge; then a wooden plank bridge and turn right on the paved road. Parallel the mountain river to State 8 and turn left. Proceed to the intersection of U.S. 276 and begin the five-mile haul to the peak. Halfway up the mountain take a breather at Bald Rock. The view here is a magnificent panorama of the valley below. Just past the summit is Raven Cliff Falls, another mountain spectacular. Five miles down the road is the North Carolina border. Follow the signs and take the road off to the right to Camp Greenville and Pretty Place, the beautiful chapel in the sky. In the one-sided chapel a rugged wooden cross is backdropped by the River Falls Valley, thousands of feet below.

After enjoying the scenery at Pretty Place, return to U.S. 276 and turn right to Cedar Mountain, North Carolina. Have lunch here at a gas station lunch counter, then retrace your route back to the campground where the Lodge serves tasty dinners.

The next morning take the same

Approximate mileage: 110, 2 tours.

Best times for touring: Late fall, when the forest is full of color.

Terrain: Back country roads that are often steep. Good bikes with very low gears are a necessity.

Traffic: Light.

Historical points of interest: Poinsett Bridge.

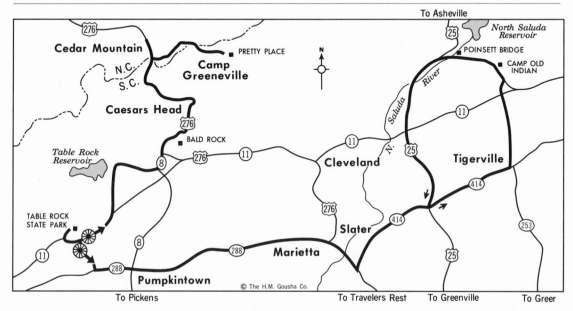

route out of the campsite to State 11 for a short distance, then pick up State Route 288. Turn left and follow 288 to Marietta. Take a right on U.S. 276 to the intersection of State 414. Go left here and follow the road to Tigerville. Turn left onto the main road toward the mountain range visible to the north. Continue to the intersection at State 11 and go across, taking a right at the next intersection up the hill. Near the top follow the signs on a very steep quarter mile to the summit. Stay on this road past Camp Old Indian and finally to Poinsett Stone Bridge, at one time the only route across the mountains.

The bridge, built in 1820, was named after Joel R. Poinsett, U.S. ambassador to Mexico who introduced the lovely red poinsettias to the United States.

After visiting the bridge continue down the steep hill out to U.S. 25 and turn left toward State 414. Turn right and retrace the route to Marietta.

Old Forts and Antique Planes on Santee Run

Antique airplanes, historic forts and the capital of South Carolina are all part of this 157-mile tour through the south.

The tour begins at Columbia, easily accessible via Interstate 20 or Interstate 26. The capital city of South Carolina, Columbia has had an interesting and turbulent history. The governing body of the state met here for the first time on January 4, 1790. Seventy-five years later during the Civil War, Gen. William T. Sherman's troops occupied the city and reduced it to ashes. After another century had passed, in 1961, Columbia had recovered so well that it was selected as one of the top ten business cities in the nation.

The tour takes State 48 southeast out of Columbia. The route is flat and makes for pleasant, relaxed cycling. **Continue through the small town** of Gadsden, the namesake of the prominent Revolutionary leader, Christopher Gadsden. At the Stamp Act Convention, Gadsden along with James Otis and Patrick Henry was violently opposed to asking any favor of the king and advocated the union of all the colonies resisting unjust taxation.

At Wateree the route takes State 267 south through Lone Star and Elloree and into Santee. This town on Lake Marion is the jump off point for some interesting side trips. Before embarking on the road to the Revolutionary War monuments you might like to warm up for your flight into the past at Santee's Wings and Wheels Museum. Antique airplanes and autos are on display and there is a taped narration of the history of transportation in the first half of the 20th century. Admission $2.

The old battle site of Fort Watson is eight miles away across Lake Marion on U.S. 15 and 301. Here, on a 48-foot mound Gen. Francis Marion attacked and captured a British fortification, its garrison, supplies and ammunition.

Approximate mileage: 156 miles, with two optional side trips.

Best times for touring: Winter and fall, when the temperatures are cooler.

Terrain: Good blacktop roads, flat for the first 25 miles, some hills near Santee.

Traffic: Not bad during winter and fall.

Historical points of interest: Fort Watson, Outlaw Springs Battlefield, Wings and Wheels Museum.

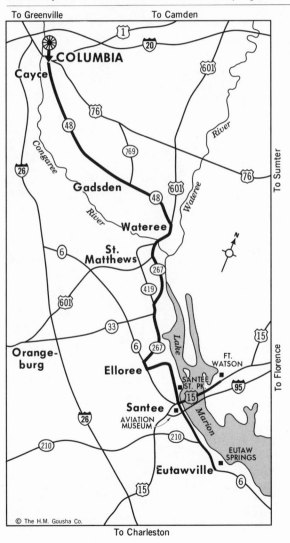

Gen. Marion was a colorful and effective leader of a motley crew of old men and boys known as "Marion's Men." Wise in the ways of guerrilla tactics, Marion, the "Swamp Fox" was the scourge of the British in South Carolina.

The other side trip is to Eutaville and Eutaw Springs Battlefield off State 6. Here was the last major engagement in the War for Independence in South Carolina. On September 8, 1781, Gen. Nathaneal Greene's troops shattered the British command and led to the British evacuation of Orangeburg, leaving the Americans in charge of the interior of the state.

There is an excellent campground at Santee State Park with hot showers and other facilities. Admission $3. Good motels and restaurants in the town.

Southeast

Bicentennial Tours of Daniel Boone Country

He may not have been quite as tall as a mountain but Daniel Boone did swing a pretty fair axe. On this tour through "Boone territory" you'll pedal through some of his handiwork as you cruise by the famed scenery of the Bluegrass Country.

The tour begins in Lexington, the "Capital of the Kingdom of the Horses." Well over 200 horse farms with thoroughbreds owned by the aristocrats of the horsey-set surround the city. You can visit many of them and horse around for free. Another sidelight is the home of the famed Kentucky politician and orator, Henry Clay, located just out of town.

Out of Lexington, head south on U.S. 25/421 through the large pastures and famous grasslands. (After Lexington there is no place for bike repairs, even tires.) About 20 miles down the road watch for the signs that lead to Whitehall State Shrine. This was the home of abolitionist leader, Cassius

Marcellus Clay, the man some historians claim was instrumental in Lincoln's presidential nomination in 1860. Clay later served under Lincoln as ambassador to Russia.

(To extend this tour continue down U.S. 25/421 to Richmond and pick up the First Kentucky Settlement ride, page 82).

Fort Boonesborough State Park is close to the Kentucky River on U.S. 627. It was here that Daniel Boone and his 30 men who helped open up the Kentucky wilderness to settlers built their stronghold in 1775. There are no visible remains of the fort but a series of plaques tell the story of the frontier. There are picnic facilities, beach and camping. The bicentennial will be celebrated in 1975. Also, up the line a bit, is the first established church west of the Appalachians, the Old Stone Meeting House, where the Boone family worshipped.

Follow the route past Winchester to

Approximate mileage: 125 round trip.

Best times for touring: April, May and October; O.K. in summer, but it is hot and humid.

Terrain: All paved two-lane country roads with rolling hills.

Traffic: Light.

Historical points of interest: Henry Clay Home, Whitehall State Shrine, Fort Boonesborough State Park, Old Stone Meeting House, Natural Bridge State Park.

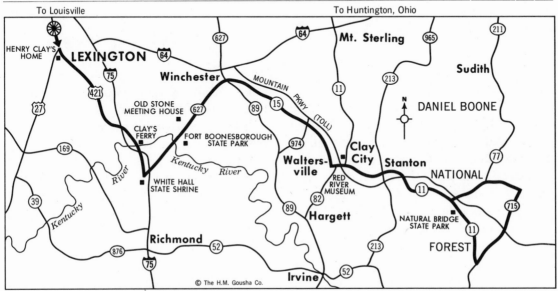

State 15 heading southeast. An interesting sidelight in Clay City, about 20 miles along this pleasant drive, is the Red River Historical Museum. On display is a collection of old tools and Indian artifacts and L.A.W. member Joe Bowen's finds on his 14,000 mile "Discover Bicycle America" tour.

After a few miles you will be in Daniel Boone National Forest. Turn left onto State 77 and loop around to pick up State 715. After several zig-zagging miles you will turn right on State 11 and follow it to Natural Bridge State Resort Park.

Nature trails lead through the high stone cliffs and arches that gave the park its name. The grandaddy of the park, Natural Bridge, has an arched opening 78 feet in length and 65 feet high. The park features a large lake, and hot buttered biscuits, Kentucky country ham and southern fried chicken at the Hemlock Lodge.

Family Tour to the First Kentucky Settlement

A fine bicycle trip for a family or individual interested in Kentucky culture and background, this tour is loaded with historical spots to visit, as well as the famed handicraft shops of Kentucky.

Before you leave Richmond go into the Madison County Court House to see a large stone found locally with Squire Boone's name and date carved on it. Squire was Daniel's brother.

The route takes State 169 out of the city. On the way to Valley View you will ride by the area where the famous Indian scout Kit Carson was born.

At Valley View you will take the ferry across the Kentucky River. The ferry has more of a distinction than just keeping your wheels dry; it's the oldest continuously operated business in Kentucky.

Now ride through Nicholasville, the home of Bluegrass Race Horse Farms.

Pick up State 29 and then U.S. 68 into Pleasant Hill. Built in 1805 by the Shakers, this restored town is now operated by young people who dress in the style of the early 1880's.

Into Harrodsburg next. Here in 1774 the first settlement in what is now Kentucky was founded. It is also the site of Kentucky's first racetrack. At Old Fort Harrod State Park just outside of town is the restored fort and log cabin where Abraham Lincoln's parents were married. There is an historic museum.

Danville is also rich in history. See Constitution Square where Kentucky's constitution was written in 1792 and visit the McDowell House.

A pleasant long ride through lovely countryside brings you into Berea, where the famous mountain college was founded in 1855. There is no tuition for needy, deserving students. They work their way through at the college industries of crafts, arts and agriculture.

There are no places to camp along the route but the motels are plentiful and the restaurants good.

Approximate mileage: 100.

Best times for touring: Late April to late October.

Terrain: Paved roads through bluegrass country; gentle hills.

Traffic: Sometimes heavy during the tourist season around Harrodsburg and Danville.

Historical points of interest: Squire Boone Rock, Valley View Ferry, Pleasant Hill, (Shaker town), Harrodsburg-first Kentucky settlement, Berea College, Danville.

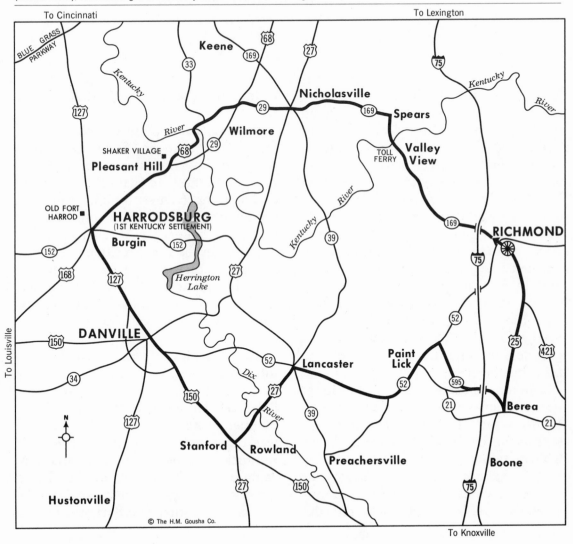

My Old Kentucky Home—Lincoln Land

Young Abraham Lincoln lore and whiskey legends are nicely blended on this 80-mile Kentucky loop tour.

Begin at Hodgenville—this is Lincoln country. In the public square is a bronze statue of the great statesman, erected in 1909. There are no campgrounds here but numerous motels are available. A few miles out of town is the Abraham Lincoln Birthplace National Historic Site. Here a great marble-and-granite memorial houses the tiny log cabin where the Civil War president was born. The Boundary Oak, over 300 years old, stands nobly on the grounds, the only living testimonial to Lincoln's birth.

The tour takes State 210 to the junction of State 470 and picks up State 84 to head east. Past Raywick the tour takes State 426 into Lebanon. St. Mary's College founded here in 1821, was the first Catholic college for boys west of the Alleghenies. There are no campgrounds here, but plenty of motels and restaurants that serve good Kentucky fare.

Pick up State 55 out of Lebanon and follow the road to Springfield. Five miles north of the town on State 528 is Lincoln Homestead State Park. Here in a compound framed by split rails is a replica of the cabin built on this spot in 1782 by an earlier Abraham Lincoln, grandfather of the President. Thomas Lincoln, father of the Great Emancipator lived here until he was 25. Further up the route off State Route 458 is Mooresville Covered Bridge, built in 1865.

The tour picks up U.S. 62 and heads into Bardstown, the second oldest city in the state. Nearby is My Old Kentucky Home State Park. Composer Stephen Foster visited here in 1852 and was inspired to write "My Old Kentucky Home," a melody that became a lasting favorite. Besides being famous in song the area is also well known for spirits. The Barton Museum

Approximate mileage: 80.

Best times for touring: April through October, but July is hot.

Terrain: Paved highways over gentle hills.

Traffic: Tourist traffic between middle June to Labor Day.

Historical points of interest: My Old Kentucky Home, Barton Museum of Whiskey History, Abraham Lincoln Birthplace National Historical Site, Lincoln Homestead State Shrine.

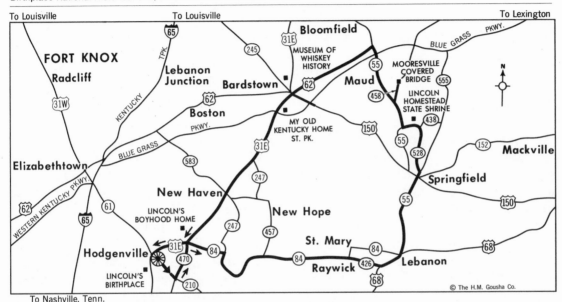

of Whiskey History chronicles the role of the heady brew from pre-Colonial days to Prohibition. A favorite display is the booz bottle, from which the slang word "booze" originated, among other drinking artifacts.

St. Joseph's Cathedral built in 1819, another landmark of the city is the first Catholic cathedral west of the Allegheny Mountains. Also, see Wickland, home of three governors, built in 1813. Campgrounds and motels are

available if you want more time to explore the town.

The tour takes U.S. 31E out of the city heading southwest. Seven miles northeast of Hodgenville you will pass Lincoln's Boyhood Home before pedaling back to the departure point.

Daniel Boone and the Derby in Bluegrass Country

The Kentucky Derby, the capital of the Bluegrass State, and a large sprinkling of Daniel Boone history are the highlights of this 75-mile round trip.

Louisville is the starting point, but actually you could start from the other end at Frankfort.

If you don't mind crowds, plan on being in Louisville during Derby Days, the ten days before the Derby is run on the first Saturday of May. Steamwheelers and spectacular parades set the festive tone before the thoroughbreds actually run. Be sure to make motel reservations far in advance—and Derby tickets, too. 1974 marks the hundredth running of the classic.

Churchill Downs is the famous home of America's best known horserace. At the main entrance at 700 Central Ave. is the Kentucky Derby Museum with displays to fortify you with historical background.

Try to find time also for the Kentucky Railway Museum, open on weekends. Among all sorts of hulking steam engines see the locomotive that pulled rough-riding Teddy Roosevelt around the country on his run for the presidency.

Now get out into the horse raising country. Ride the route through rolling grasslands to Shelbyville. Here is a landmark that should spark a bit of pride in any senior citizen who believes Horatio Alger wasn't a fake. This is the home of that finger lickin' father of fried fowl, Colonel Sanders, who at the age of 65, founded the Kentucky Fried Chicken empire.

Continue down U.S. 60/460 to the capital of Kentucky at Frankfort. The city, the head of the state's government since 1792, contains many buildings connected with the history of Kentucky. The Capitol Building, completed in 1910, is of classic design with an elegance fitting for these hospitable southern folks. Murals in the building depict some history of the state.

Approximate mileage: 75, round trip.

Best times for touring: April through October.

Terrain: Hilly in places, but not steep, good two-lane, paved roads.

Traffic: Local, some heavier traffic coming out of Louisville.

Historical points of interest: Boone's Grave, Governor's Mansion, State Capitol, Kentucky Historical Museum, Churchill Downs, Jefferson County Court House.

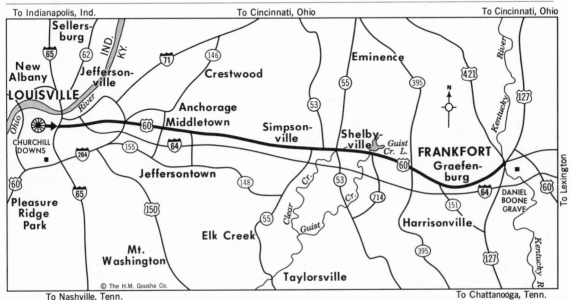

Outside on the Capitol grounds the Great Floral Clock, its face filled with 20,000 blooms, keeps perfect time with hands weighing half-a-ton spinning around a dial 34 feet wide.

The Old Governor's Mansion is a unique blend of history and elegance. The house, home for 33 governors between 1798 and 1914, has been restored to the dignity and beauty of the 18th century. The house now serves as the residence of lieutenant governors.

Daniel Boone and his wife Rebecca are buried at the Frankfort cemetery, overlooking the valley the frontier explorer visited on one of his first visits to the Kentucky wilderness. A "Boone Tour," marked by signs leads through many unusual sights including the "Corner of Celebrities," consisting of the square formed by Wapping, Washington, Main and Wilkinson streets. It is believed that more distinguished men lived in those four acres than on any similar plot of land in the United States.

Touring the Foothills of the Great Smokies

This 50-mile-plus tour that takes in the Smoky Mountain foothills is easy on the eyes, offering spectacular mountain scenery, and not too hard on the legs as the pathway isn't steep.

The tour begins in Maryville, a Tennessee town where Samuel Houston once taught school.

Start from State Route 73 out of Maryville to the Foothills Parkway. From here there is a rewarding side trip to Cades Cove. Continue on State Route 73 and enter the Great Smoky Mountain National Park (the only time the tour actually passes through the park) about two miles past Townsend. The tour is a one way loop, 10 miles mostly uphill to the Cove campground through hardwood forests and stands of conifers that have been called "a piece of Canada stranded in the Smokies." Then, a fast cruise back over the same route. The road winds past pioneer homesteads, old frame churches, and the Cable Mill, where corn is ground as it was a century ago.

Back down to the Foothills Parkway, the route follows the base of the majestic Smokies to U.S. 129.

The site of the pre-Revolutionary British stronghold at Fort Loudoun offers a worthwhile stopping place.

The fort was built by the colony of South Carolina in 1756 as Great Britain's southwestern outpost in the French and Indian War. It strengthened the friendship of the Cherokee tribe, who, with the British, were checking the French advance in the south while the English captured French strongholds in the north.

Later, in 1760, hostilities between the Cherokees and the British became so severe that the Indians blockaded the fort. In early August of that year, Fort Loudoun surrendered.

To complete the tour it is possible to get back to Maryville via U.S. 411 but the traffic is heavy. The better route would be to return to State 115.

Approx. mileage: 55; side trip to Cades Cove, 20.

Best times for touring: Spring and fall.

Terrain: Foothills of the Smoky Mountains, easy hills except for the steeper climb to Cades Cove.

Traffic: Heavy on U.S. 411.

Historical points of interest: Site of Fort Loudon.

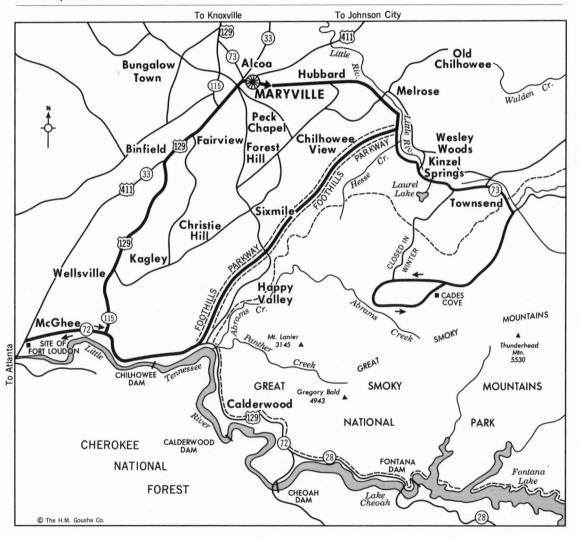

Follow the Indian Path on the Old Natchez Trace

The Natchez Trace Parkway is the location of a ride through this beautiful historic land of Indians, explorers and frontiersmen.

The route begins south of Nashville at Gordonsburg and extends 60 miles along the northern part of the 306-mile Parkway. The Parkway roughly follows the path of the Old Natchez Trace. The Trace began as a network of beaten paths, probably first made by deer or buffalo. Later the Indians used the trails for warpaths, hunting routes and transportation between villages.

Evidence of prehistoric Indians: mounds, shell heaps, fortifications, cemeteries and village sites still abound along the Trace. From its apparent age and origin the route derived its name—trace in old French meant a trail made from footprints or animal tracks.

The French were the first Europeans to explore the area. They came as early as 1699 and settled in Natchez in 1716. The colony prospered but was later destroyed by a Natchez Indian massacre that killed nearly 300 people. French traders, missionaries and soldiers frequently traveled the many links of the Trace.

The French in 1763 ceded the region to the British, who settled the area and held it until after the American Revolution. As the result of the British defeat, Spain claimed the land. In 1798, Spain surrendered the area to the U.S.

The northern part of the Trace, near the route you will follow on this tour, had a less violent history. The British began trading in the area around 1700 but no permanent settlement was made until North Carolinians founded Nashville in 1780.

The blessing of the Trace is the lack of commercial activity; unfortunately like all blessings it has its curse, there are no places to buy food or repairs for your bike. Bring edibles and a repair kit.

Just outside Gordonsburg is Meri-

Approximate mileage: 60, one way.

Best times for touring: Spring or fall.

Terrain: Easy grades.

Traffic: No problem.

Historical points of interest: Meriwether Lewis Park, the Trace, Indian Mounds.

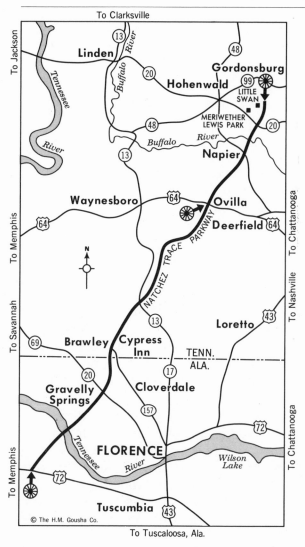

wether Lewis Park, where the great explorer is buried. There is a museum nearby with an account of his life. Also nearby is Metal Ford and Napier Mine where you can get a close look and frontier mining and smelting.

(An enjoyable way to ride the Trace with a group is to break up the tour by dropping off half the party at Ovilla, on U.S. 64, and driving the rest north to the starting point at Gordonsburg. The first group will ride to the end of the tour in Alabama at U.S. 72; then return and meet the second group for the trip back to Gordonsburg.)

The section of the Trace south to Tupelo is incomplete. See page 92 for the Trace tour from Tupelo south to Jackson, Mississippi.

Try the Mississippi Leg of Natchez Trace

Pedal down a leisurely road into the past on this 150-mile tour along the historic Natchez Trace Parkway in Mississippi.

The parkway follows roughly crossing, recrossing and at times paralleling, the route of the Old Natchez Trace. A frontier road in early American history, the Trace eventually linked the Old Southwest with the more developed East. (See pages 90-91 for another Trace tour.)

Today, markers, exhibits and trails explain the varied and turbulent history of this stomping ground of Indians, explorers and traders.

The tour begins at Tupelo, accessible via U.S. 45 from the north or south, U.S. 78 from the east or State Route 6 from the west.

Before starting it might be wise to stop in at the Tupelo Visitor Center. Here you can get an overview of the parkway by seeing the film "Path of Empire." Also you can check on the rules and regulations of the area.

Two places you might like to see before hitting the trail are the Brices Cross Roads National Battlefield Site north of Tupelo and the Tupelo National Battlefield Site just outside of town.

Brices Cross Roads was designated as a memorial to Gen. Nathan Bedford Forrest's victory over Union forces on June 10, 1864. The victory was hailed as an important Confederate conquest, but in reality it achieved a major Union goal by keeping Forrest away from Gen. Sherman's supply line in Tennessee.

About 15 miles out of Tupelo along the parkway is Bynum Mounds where exhibits, markers and trails remind you that this was the land of Choctaw, Chickasaw and prehistoric Indians.

Another 20 miles further is Jeff Busby Park. There is a campground here and a nice view from the highest elevation on the parkway in Mississippi.

Past Hurricane Creek in the town of Kosciusko was the site where Andrew

Approx. mileage: 150, one way.

Best times for touring: Spring or fall, too hot during the summer.

Terrain: Relaxed cycling over a paved road.

Traffic: No commercial traffic allowed on the route, so traffic moderate.

Historical points of interest: Markers and sites all along the trail; Civil War battle sites in Tupelo.

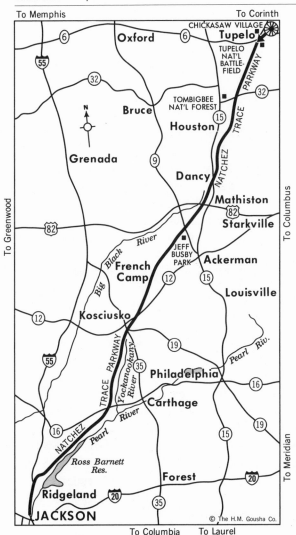

Jackson camped during the War of 1812. On the miserable homeward march the tough commander kept his sick army alive with rations of horse meat, and earned the nickname "Old Hickory."

The route continues past Beaver Dam through Ridgeland, which has interesting exhibits, and finally into Jackson, named after the military leader.

Jackson, the capitol of Mississippi, also preserves the history of the Natchez Trace in museum exhibits displayed in the old Mississippi State Capitol, now restored.

Recycle the Roads of Chickamauga Battlefield

Cyclists can choose any of the roads winding through the Chickamauga battle site in Georgia but it is helpful to start at the Visitor Center to pick up maps and historical background that will make the ride more meaningful. The tour traced here is about 13 miles long but there are 27 miles of good, paved roads in all throughout the park. Try to avoid U.S. 27 when possible, as the traffic is heavy at times.

The wooded park is especially lovely in the spring and colorful in the fall, with many good picnic sites. (There are also good restaurants on U.S. 27 toward Chattanooga and many motels in the area.) The National Park Service gives a special warning about poison ivy. Watch where you put yourself and your bike!

The battle of Chickamauga got underway hurriedly on September 18, 1863, and for the next two days Union and Confederate soldiers struggled through the massive undergrowth.

The situation at dawn on September 19 found the two armies facing each other along the banks of Chickamauga Creek. Near Jay's Mill, reconnoitering forces from both sides met and the battle began.

Fighting on the second day was slow to get underway and lasted until nightfall in a fierce engagement on Snodgrass Hill.

The Confederates won the great battle of Chickamauga with a price of 18,000 lives. The tally on the Union side was 16,000.

The defeat for Union forces was melancholy. But, sections of the army managed to get back to Chattanooga, where they remained under siege for weeks. Gradually, resupplying and reinforcing of the Union army took place.

Finally, in late November at Gen. Grant's orders, the Union met and defeated the Confederate forces in the sieges of Lookout Mountain and Missionary Ridge.

Approximate mileage: up to 27.

Best times for touring: Fall and spring.

Terrain: Mostly flat and wooded. Paved roads; U.S. 27 has good shoulders.

Traffic: Avoid heavily traveled U.S. 27.

Historical points of interest: Chickamauga National Military Park, nearby Missionary Ridge, Lookout Mountain.

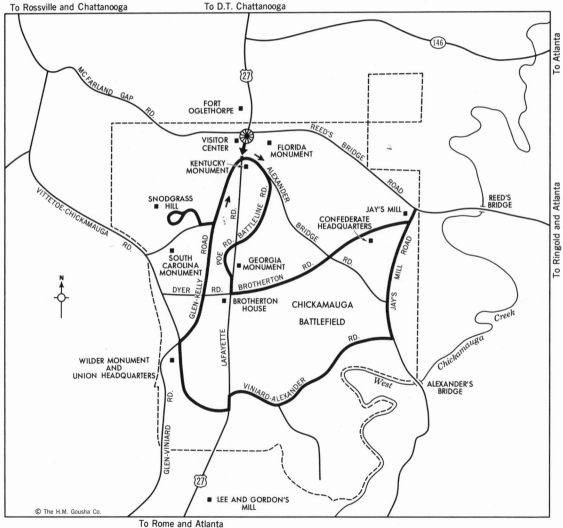

From a Space Center to Paint Rock River

This Alabama tour contrasts technology with nature as the cyclist travels from the eerieness of a space center to the tranquility of a river.

The tour can begin either in Huntsville or Paint Rock. Either way you will probably pass through Huntsville, an Alabama city that combines the old and the new.

Situated on the site of a curving valley, Huntsville is the home of the first constitutional convention of the Alabama Territory. The convention met in 1819 and set the guidelines for the new state. Many stately houses of that era still stand; an odd contrast to the city's new image as a space center.

On July 1, 1960, in Huntsville, the George Marshall Space Flight Center of NASA began operations. The center designed and tested the Redstone and Saturn missiles, created and launched the first American satellites, accomplished the first flight into space and recovery of animal life, and the safe completion of the first manned space flights of the United States.

At the Space Orientation Center are exhibits which include "Spin-Offs from Space", an explanation of the benefits to mankind resulting from space research, a moon rock display and space movies. Open daily, Sunday after 1 p.m., there is no admission.

Out of Huntsville the tour takes U.S. 72 to Paint Rock. This is a rather large throughway so be careful of cars and the wind from passing trucks.

At Paint Rock the route heads north on State 65. From here the tour follows the Paint Rock River which derived its name from a large rock at the river's confluence with the Tennessee River that boatmen used as a navigation marker.

All along the river are excellent places for a picnic lunch. The route continues north through Trenton, Princeton and finally concludes at Estillfork.

Approximate mileage: From Huntsville 76; from Paint Rock, 40.

Best times for touring: Hot in the summer, more pleasant in the spring or fall.

Terrain: Good secondary roads, 40 miles along Paint Rock River.

Traffic: Some heavy trucks on U.S. 72.

Historical points of interest: Space Orientation Center.

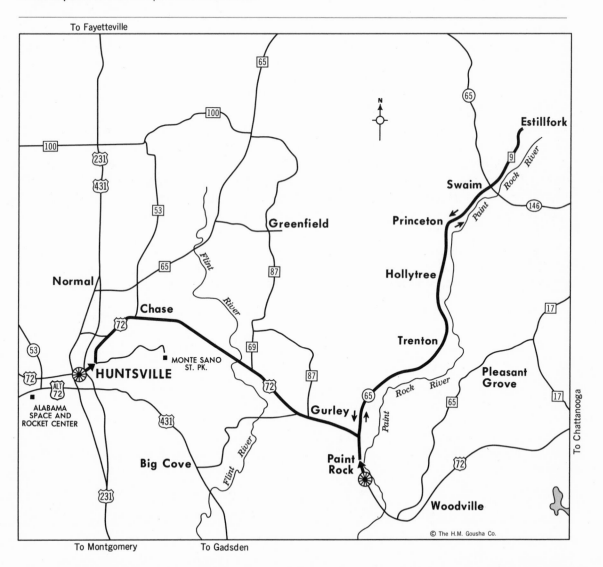

"Damn the Torpedoes" Tour to Fort Gaines

An easy 37 mile, one-way jaunt along Mobile Bay, this tour is excellent for the cyclist who likes to travel at a leisurely pace and view some interesting side-lights. If you plan to spend time sightseeing you should arrange for a ride one way by car.

The tour begins in Mobile, easily reached from Interstate 10.

Mobile is noted for its tree-lined boulevards, old mansions, grillwork balconies and lovely gardens. It's also well-known for its annual Mardi Gras before Easter, and Azalea Trail Festival in February and March, when the blooms are at their best.

Leave Mobile on U.S. 90 (Government St.) and take State 163 south along Mobile Bay.

About five miles from Mobile is Clarke Gardens. This scenic sanctuary is alive with colors in the spring and fall when the flowers and trees tantalize the eyes and nose. Children are admitted free but adult nature lovers have to produce their own greenery, $1.

The bayside ride continues down State 163. A Bellingrath Gardens side trip is an option at County Rd. 22. Off Rd. 22 turn left on Rd. 59 and again left to the famous gardens. Thousands of showy flowering shrubs bank the Ile-aux-Olies River as it winds through many acres of the huge gardens. This is azalea country—over 250,000 plants of 200 varieties. Travels to world-famous gardens abroad inspired industrialist W.D. Bellingrath and his wife to consult a French gardener, an English landscape designer and other experts. You may tour the garden with a guide or by the free map provided. Admission; open daily.

The regular tour continues along State Route 163 to the Gordon Persons Overseas Highway and over the water to Dauphin Island.

When the French landed here in 1699 they found human bones bleaching on the sands and dubbed the place

Approx. mileage: 37, one way; Bellingrath Gardens, additional 8.

Best time for touring: Spring or summer.

Terrain: Flat, easy road.

Traffic: Moderate.

Historical points of interest: Fort Gaines, old mansions, Clarke Gardens, Bellingrath Gardens.

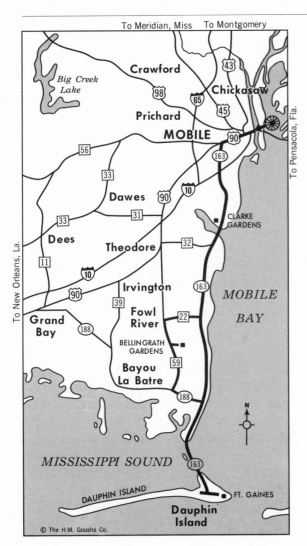

Massacre Island. The Island has progressed from those macabre days to a sunbather's haven along the salt sprayed stretch of beach.

During the Civil War, Admiral David G. Farragut, ordered to capture Mobile, sailed his flagship, the *Hartford*, into Mobile Bay. The guns from Dauphin Island's Fort Gaines faced him from the left and Fort Morgan's artillery was aimed from the right. Additionally, five rows of explosives-rigged pilings, then known as torpedoes, blocked his path. When one of his ships was hit by a torpedo and sunk, Farragut barked his famous "Damn the torpedoes" command and pressed the attack in spite of the odds. Within four days Farragut had Union flags waving over Fort Gaines, Morgan, and Mobile Bay.

On the tip of Dauphin Island you can visit the confederate museum at the still standing Fort Gaines. Near the bastion's entry the anchor and chain from the *Hartford* stand as reminders of the grim battle.

Century Run From Panama City to Pensacola

Bikinis, sun and white sands highlight this tour down Florida's Gulf of Mexico coast. Besides the bikinis there are some interesting historical sidelights. Grab some suntan lotion and a hat and you're ready for a century run from Panama City to Pensacola.

The tour begins in Panama City, but can be reversed with the starting point at Pensacola.

Panama City has been favorably compared to Atlantic City; both have the roller coasters and convention hall, but the fishing is better in Florida.

To get on the road take the bridge over St. Andrews Bay to U.S. 98. You'll be right along the Gulf now, passing beaches and resorts.

On this first leg of the trip you may want to relax on one of the main beaches. Sunnyside, the last one before you leave the coast for awhile on U.S. 98, is a good spot for a snack and beach lounging. (You can stay next to the Gulf on State 30A just north of Sunnyside.)

About 35 miles past Sunnyside is Destin. This is an excellent overnight stopover before continuing to Pensacola.

Just up the highway is Fort Walton Beach. Once noted mainly for its beaches and water sports, the city has taken a turn to the past and has gained recognition for its archaeological excavations.

At Temple Mound and Museum, right on U.S. 98, downtown, is an excavated mound that once served as a major religious and civic center for Indian tribes of the area. Artifacts from civilizations which existed here in prehistoric times have been uncovered. The Mound is open daily and is free.

For an interesting side trip cross over to Santa Rosa Island on State 399 about 15 miles past Fort Walton. Continue down this route past Pensacola Beach to Fort Pickens.

The Confederates who held Pensacola in 1862 ordered the Federals to

Approximate mileage: 109, one way.

Best times for touring: All year around, but an ideal winter tour.

Traffic: Heavy near cities.

Terrain: A long, flat strip of highway adjacent to white sand beaches.

Historical points of interest: Fort Pickens, Temple Mound Indian excavations.

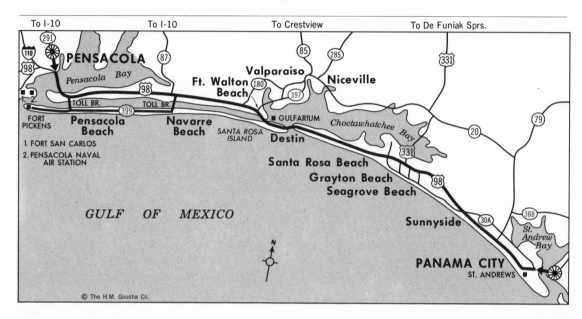

surrender Fort Pickens or face the consequences, which they did. The fort eventually wound up as a prison, having Geronimo as its most famous inmate.

To get back on the main route ride to the toll bridge at Pensacola Beach and pick up U.S. 98 into the city. Pensacola has had a turbulent history. Don Tristan de Luna landed an expedition of 1,500 here in 1559, six years before the founding of St. Augustine. Unfor-

tunately a storm destroyed De Luna's fleet two years later, and the settlement was abandoned.

Good accommodations in Pensacola, as well as the Wentworth Museum and Art Center.

St. Augustine and the Buccaneer Trail

The northeastern coast of Florida lends itself to three tours, all of which are suitable for weekend jaunts or one-day excursions if you can arrange for transportation to eliminate the return rides.

This is a very historic section of Florida, and you'll have plenty of opportunities to stop, visit museums and forts, and take pictures. Add to this the natural beach attractions, and you have an ideal recreation area.

At the northern tip of the route is Fort Clinch State Park, site of a great brick fort built in 1850–60. Amelia Island, with its strategic position at the mouth of the St. Mary's River, has been held by Spanish, French, British, Confederate and American governments during the past two centuries.

In Amelia City is the Palace Saloon, Florida's oldest bar. The interior is a conglomeration of international craftsmanship. A few miles south you begin the Buccaneer Trail, a toll road.

On Sundays, bicyclers may tour aircraft carriers and other vessels in port at the Mayport Naval Air Station.

Kingsley House on Fort George Island, is considered the oldest plantation in Florida. The house was built in 1817 by one of Florida's most colorful pioneers, Zephaniah Kingsley.

As the oldest permanent settlement in the United States, St. Augustine is worth as much time as you can spare. There are many restored houses and museums open to the public, and you may enjoy just riding through the side streets to look at the old walled gardens, plazas and curious combination of old and new architectural styles. Keep an eye on traffic, though, since many of the back streets are very narrow and crowded.

Fourteen miles south of St. Augustine is Fort Matanzas, where Spanish slaughtered all the French survivors of a hurricane-wrecked fleet attacking St. Augustine.

Approximate mileage: 122 for the entire one-way trip; 120-mile round trips between Fernandina Beach and St. Augustine, and St. Augustine and Daytona Beach.

Best times for touring: All year.

Terrain: Mostly flat.

Traffic: Can be heavy in popular beach areas, St. Augustine and Daytona Beach.

Historical points of interest: St. Augustine, oldest city in the U.S., Palace Saloon, many forts.

To Savannah, Ga.

To Waycross, Ga.

FT. CLINCH ST. PK.
Fernandina Beach
Amelia City

ATLANTIC

JACKSON-VILLE

Fort George

Jacksonville Beach

OCEAN

SAINT
AUGUSTINE

BUTLER
ST. PK.

FT. MATANZAS
NAT'L MON.

MARINELAND OF FLORIDA

Palatka

WASHINGTON OAKS
GARDENS ST. PK.

Flagler Beach

BULOW PLANTATION RUINS

ADDISON BLOCKHOUSE

Ormond Beach

DAYTONA
BEACH

SEA ZOO

GREEN
MOUND

© The H.M. Gousha Co.

To Orlando   To Titusville

Bulow Plantation Ruins, near Flagler Beach, was the site of the one of the area's largest sugar plantations in the early 1800's.

Addison Blockhouse in Ormond Beach originally was an early 19th century kitchen. Seminole Indians burned both the house and the pantry in 1836, but the remnants were put to use as an earthworks by South Carolina troops defending Fort Duncan McCrea.

The Daytona Beach area is excellent for bike riding. Motorbike, beach cart and surfboard rentals are available for a change of pace. Daytona also has a boardwalk, complete with carnival atmosphere and band shell.

A Bounty of Sights on the Tampa Bay Run

Varied sightseeing pleasures along with a promise of Florida sunshine should make for a pleasant day on this tour along Tampa Bay.

St. Petersburg is noted as a city for older folks and it is true that some 25 percent of the residents are past the retirement age. But around here the oldsters don't sit, so don't be surprised if a so-called "senior citizen" whizzes by you on his bike.

The younger set have been finding a haven here also. A modern system of causeways (you'll ride on one) has made the beaches easy to reach and has offered an access to islands to the south, such as Mullet Key, an extensive recreation area.

According to which historian you believe, Ponce de Leon did or did not land on one of the islands in the Mullet Keys in 1513 and get into a fight with the Indians. He returned in 1521, was wounded in his second battle with the natives, and died, supposedly from his injuries, later in Havana.

The tour begins in the parking lot of the St. Petersburg Historical Museum at 335 Second Ave. The museum exhibits cover natural history, science, shells, Americana and even has a 3,000 year old mummy. Open daily, Sunday after 2 p.m. the admission is 75 cents.

Nearby at the Municipal Pier is MGM's replica of the 1789 mutiny ship, and the one used in the movie, "Mutiny on the Bounty." It is permanently anchored here after logging more than 50,000 miles. Open daily. Admission to the boat and a Tahitian village recreation with dioramas is $1.50.

The tour heads south from the *Bounty* on Beach Drive. Near the Albert Whitted Airport get on Third Street through Barlett Park to Sixth Street. Then over to Fourth out to Pt. Pinellas where you take a right on Pinellas Point Drive. Continue along the route past Maximo Park to the Pinellas Bayway. This is a toll road and you'll have to

Approximate mileage: 40, round trip.	

Best times for touring: All year.

Traffic: Medium.

Terrain: No grades, good roads, sometimes strong winds off the ocean.

Historical points of interest: *H.M.S. Bounty* replica, Historical Museum, Fort De Soto.

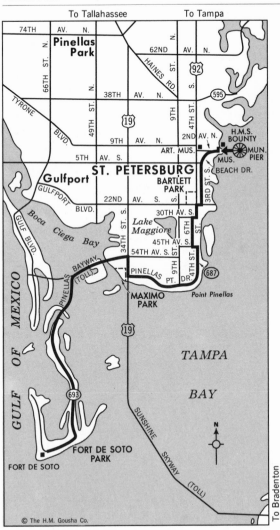

pay 60 cents. Continue along this road out to Fort de Soto Park. Take a right on State Route 693 and ride less than a mile to Fort De Soto.

The fort was begun in 1898 to protect the Tampa area during the Spanish American War, but the war ended before the work was completed. The guns that were never used are still in place. Here now is a popular recreational spot with a miniature railroad (50 cents), boating, water skiing, picnic grills, swimming, fishing piers and a cafe for a hungry cyclist.

After a refreshing swim, a cool drink and some food, the tour can be completed by taking the same route back to the *Bounty*.

Kennedy Space Center Ride on Florida's Coast

This ride up Florida's East Coast takes you to some of the state's oldest and most modern historical centers.

You can start at Stuart or drive out on Hutchinson Island before beginning the ride. There are two good stops right at the south end of the island. Elliott Museum houses a collection of antique automobiles and an exhibition of Indian and early American culture. The House of Refuge is a museum of sea lore.

St. Lucie Museum north of Fort Pierce is another good museum, this one housing a collection of treasure that has been collected off the nearby reefs, and an exhibit of U.S. Mint gold coins.

If you're riding this route in the spring, you may find the Los Angeles Dodgers in town at Vero Beach, taking spring training before opening the regular National League Season. In summer, there's another attraction—the giant sea turtles struggle up to the sun baked sands to lay their eggs. The ride north of here takes you through the rolling sand dunes mantled with seagrapes and palmettos.

If you want to cut this trip in half, Sebastian Inlet is a good stopping place before you turn back. This is one of Florida's most beautiful coastal scenes. There are campgrounds if you want to spend the night, and the fishing and diving are excellent. Offshore are wrecked ships of the Spanish Fleet, which have yielded several million dollars to treasure hunters in the past ten years. Gold coins even have been found on the beach.

Farther north, you can rent surfboards, rafts, etc., in the shops that line the beaches throughout this area. If you have a camera with you, look for the missile display in front of the Tech Lab at Patrick Air Force Base. This is supposed to be the most photographed exhibit in the entire state.

The Pineda Causeway (State 404) is a beautiful route, crossing the Banana

Approximate mileage: 100 one way, 50 to Sebastian Inlet.

Best times for touring: All year.

Terrains: Flat, with rolling sand dunes.

Traffic: Heavy near Kennedy Space Center; near beaches on weekends.

Historical points of interest: Elliot Museum, 1875 House of Refuge, St. Lucie State Museum, wrecked Spanish ships, Kennedy Space Center.

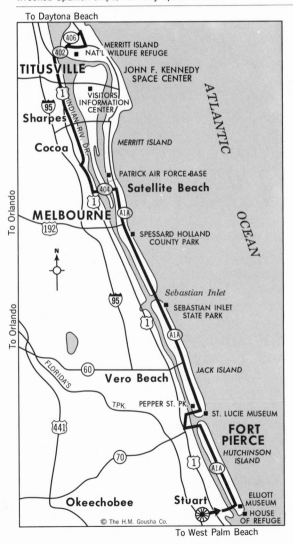

River and Indian River on arched bridges.

Indian River Drive is another of Florida's very scenic roads. The river is dotted with small islands, perfect spots for a picnic, swim or even overnight camping.

The northern tip of this ride is Merritt Island National Wildlife Refuge, where the space industry and wildlife live side by side. If you have extra time, be sure to take one of the Kennedy Space Center tours. The Center is open from 8 a.m. to sunset, and bus tours originate at the Visitor Information Center, accessible only through Gate 3. There's a Space Age Museum, displays of models and space hardware, space science lectures and space-related movies in two theaters.

Cane River Tour– The Louisiana Purchase

Natchitoches and the Cane River country are definitely part of the Old South. Natchitoches is the oldest settlement in the original Louisiana Purchase, and its romantic traditions are reminiscent of the old steamboat days. Be sure to see the Church of Immaculate Conception, Trinity Episcopal Church, and the Wells Home in East Natchitoches, one of the oldest buildings in all of northern Louisiana.

To be best appreciated, the Cane River country should be explored leisurely, and a bike ride is the best way. It might make you feel even better to know that Davey Crockett, Sam Houston, Jefferson Davis, U.S. Grant, Robert E. Lee and other heroes worked their way up this stream in centuries past.

Leave Natchitoches on Highway 1, and ride left as the highway turns at the old wooden bridge. Leave the highway where it makes a sharp turn to the right and continue straight ahead on the Cane River Road. (The longer tour shown on the map takes you down to Derry on the east side of the river, with a return trip on the west side. For an optional tour, cross the River at Melrose and start the return ride.)

The Achille Prudhomme House was built about 1840 by slave labor. It lies at the end of a long avenue of live oaks. This is what is known as a raised cottage, with a brick first floor and a wood second floor. The frame work is all hand-cut cypress.

Construction of the Oakland Plantation started in 1818, and it was enlarged to its present size about 1835. The live oaks that line the road leading to the house were brought from southern Mississippi and planted in the 1820's.

The Narcisse Prudhomme House was built in 1830. From the front, you can see three French doors that open on the 84-foot gallery. The floor and adobe walls are the originals; the rest of the building was restored in 1849.

Approximate mileage: 51 for the whole trip; cut to 37 by crossing the river at Melrose.

Best times for touring: Excellent in spring and fall.

Terrain: Flat but winding along the river's banks.

Traffic: Generally light.

Historical points of interest: Homes and plantations.

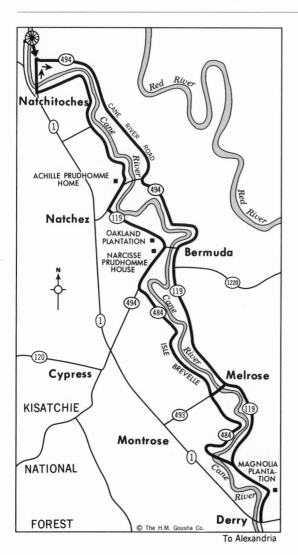

To Alexandria

Melrose is the largest privately owned pecan plantation in the world, and one of the oldest plantations in the Southwest. Yucca, the residence in the Melrose gardens, is heralded as the birthplace of many famous blacks. The African Buildings are classed as among the thirteen unique buildings of the Old South and the country's only example of African architecture dating from the colonial period.

Magnolia Plantation was built shortly after the Civil War. Brick slave cabins can still be seen behind the house.

Isle Brevelle began in the 18th century as a sanctuary for the children of white planters and their slaves. It is now a busy agricultural community, centered around St. Augustine Church, which was built in 1806.

Louisiana Ante Bellum Houses in Cajun Country

The Teche Country is a mixture of French, Spanish and Acadian cultures. Many inhabitants still speak French as well as English. New Iberia dates back to 1779, and is often called The Queen City of the Teche. This makes ideal touring country; spring is flower season, and some of the famous homes and gardens are open to the public year around. If you like to eat, watch for the creole and seafood kitchens.

You can start all the tours shown here at Longfellow-Evangeline State Park. (The Evangeline Oak is the spot where Evangeline met Gabriel as written by Longfellow.) To the south, you have two options—a straight line up-and-back ride to Avery Island (38 miles) or the 46-mile loop that takes you to more historical sites.

Avery Island is a popular tourist spot in this part of the state; it is most famous for its Jungle Gardens, but also has a salt mine, oil field, and many acres of peppers used in making the fiery, famous Tabasco Sauce.

New Iberia has many points of interest, including Shadows-On-The-Teche House museum, the 150-year-old Gebert Oak, a beautiful city park, and ante bellum houses. About three miles east of town are Justine, a restored house, and the Justine Bottle Museum, built entirely of Louisiana cypress. Loreauville Heritage Museum Village traces the area's history over the past 300 years. St. Martinville seems dedicated to preserving the best of Acadian language, customs and handicrafts.

To the north, you also have two options: a 38-mile loop, or a longer ride that covers 51 miles. Highlight of either ride is the Live Oak Trail. Farther north, the levee road is gravel, so take extra care.

Pine and Oak Alley is a double row of trees extending from the banks of the bayou to the site of a famous old plantation. It is here that plantation owner Charles Durand sprayed spider

Approximate mileage: Four tours, ranging from 38 to 51 miles.

Best times for touring: Springtime offers the best weather.

Terrain: Mostly flat.

Traffic: Can be a problem on main roads, but light on country roads.

Historical points of interest: Many historic buildings dating from early 1800's.

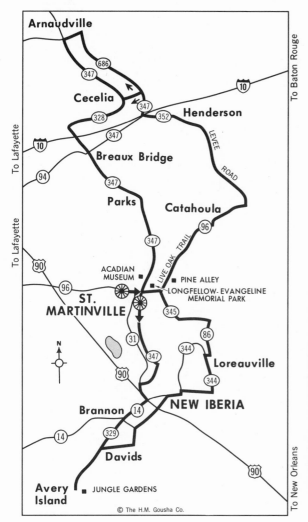

webs with gold and silver dust to help celebrate the double wedding of his daughters.

Locals claim that Pat's restaurant in Henderson has the best Cajun food for miles around.

On the return loop, you'll find Breaux Bridge, a picturesque Acadian town known locally as the "Crayfish Capital of the World."

St. John Plantation dates back to 1828, and is still in operation. It's not open to the public, but it affords passing cyclists a rare opportunity to see a complete plantation.

Midwest

Lakefront Exploring in Northern Michigan

This is part of a 250-mile tour organized in 1971 by Jerry Mason and ridden by an intrepid band of cyclists who braved rain and wind for a ride of immense beauty. The sections here are among the most manageable for cyclists with lesser appetites.

This part of northern Michigan is a classic combination of dense woods and vast expanses of water. Crowds are almost nonexistent and cyclists often have roads to themselves. Be prepared for wet weather at any time. If you have proper clothing, you can often outride a blustery squall.

Leland can be the start of an 80-mile loop trip to Traverse City, or a 100-mile, one-way ride to East Jordan. On either ride, you're in sight of Lake Michigan a good part of the way, and the weather and wind are constant reminders of the marine influence.

Leland is on the scenic Leelanau Peninsula, and the circle route takes you up to the tip and back down to the base at Traverse City. For the return ride, you can retrace your steps or turn inland and cross the peninsula at Lake Leelanau.

Traverse City is important in the country's history as a major producer of cherries. The town started in 1847 as a timber town, but small plantings of fruit did so well that the area soon devoted itself to agriculture. There is a fine park in town with a zoo of native Michigan animals, beach concessions, and a museum of pioneer and Indian exhibits.

A very popular scenic ride in this area extends north on Old Mission Peninsula along Highway 37. Right at the tip is a spot supposedly located equal distances from the North Pole and the equator.

North from Traverse City, you follow a country road that passes along the east side of Torch Lake before turning east into East Jordan where there are motels and restaurants.

Approximate mileage: Leland-Traverse City round trip, 80; one-way ride, Leland to East Jordan, 100.

Best times for touring: Summer, in warm weather.

Terrain: North woods, lake front, but no really steep grades.

Traffic: For the most part, light.

Historical points of interest: Traverse City.

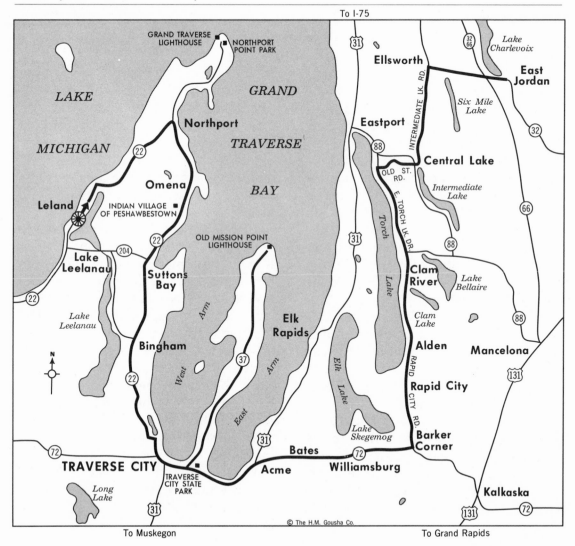

Investigate the Mystery of the Mounds Builders

The traces of Ohio's earliest and most mysterious race, the Mound Builders, highlight this Buckeye State tour.

Either end of the tour is a good starting place. If you begin in Chillicothe, there is a campground, Fleshman's Dogwood circle, nine miles east on Choalestor Pikes. Chillicothe was the first capital of the Northwest Territory and became the first capital of Ohio in 1803. Just out of town off U.S. 50 is the Ross County Historical Society Museum containing pioneer crafts, rifle making information, and historical material on the Mound Builders. If you suffer from mansion mania, this city has a good one. The Adena State Memorial, a 22-room mansion of Thomas Worthington, sixth governor of Ohio, is an elegant structure enhanced by towering Mt. Logan looming in the background. The city is also the home of the *Gazette,* the oldest continually published paper west of the Allegheny Mountains.

Pedaling down U.S. 50 the next stop is the Seip Mound State Memorial. Here the prehistoric burial mound, 250 feet long and 30 feet high, is surrounded by fascinating smaller mounds and earthworks. Picnic facilities are available.

At Bainbridge along the route see the Dental Museum on Main Street. Here in the small building, Dr. John Harris founded the first dental school in America. Near here are the Seven Caves, where cliffs, canyons and waterfalls surround illuminated caves.

At Locust Grove the route heads northwest on State Route 73 for four miles to the Serpent Mound State Memorial. This is one of the greatest works of the Mound Builders. Like a snake peering from the past, the mound lies coiled on a rocky plateau. Over 1,300 feet long and 20 feet wide, the serpent seems to protect an oval figure in the cavern of its gaping jaws. Because of the deep ravines and heavy

Approximate mileage: 127.

Best times for touring: April through May.

Terrain: Some hills but mostly gentle rolling country highways.

Traffic: No problem.

Historical points of interest: Chillicothe, Seip Mount State Memorial, Serpent Mound State Memorial, Fort Ancient State Memorial, Miamisburg Mound State Memorial.

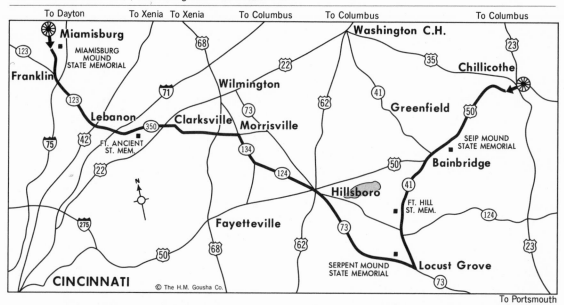

forest here and in surrounding areas, cycling shutterbugs will do best between 11 a.m. and 2 p.m.

The tour continues up State 73 past Hillsboro to State Routes 124 and 134. Motel accommodations are available in Hillsboro.

Now you pick up State 350 and head west to Fort Ancient State Memorial. One hundred acres are enclosed here by an earth wall that guards the Fort Ancient Indian Community. The museum houses displays and explanations.

Up the road along State 123 is Lebanon. The Glendover State Memorial in town is a beautifully restored Greek revival mansion built by Milton Williams in 1836. There are motels in town and a campground one mile east off State Route 123 on Stubbs Mill Road.

The route heads north to Miamisburg and the end of the Indian Mound adventure. The last stop is the Miamisburg Mound State Memorial with the largest conical mound in Ohio.

Visit the Presidents on this Ohio Century

Two U.S. Presidents made their home along this route and the heritage they left highlights this Ohio centuryride. This is an easy ride, ideal for those who like a large dose of scenery and sightseeing with their mileage.

The tour begins in Columbus of Int. 70 (But you also can start in Findlay.) The capital of Ohio, the city is brimming with places to visit.

The Ohio state capitol is home to bronze statues of famous statesmen; including Grant, Sherman, Garfield, Hayes and others. The Ohio Historical Center contrasts modern architectural and museum design with the age-old themes of Ohio's prehistoric culture. Another must stop is Ohio State University, one of the ten largest in the country with museums and art galleries. A tour of the campus is well worth hopping off the bike.

Out of Columbus the tour takes State Route 315 north. Visit the Perkins Observatory, if you happen to be in the area between 2 and 3 p.m. and look through the 32 inch reflecting telescope. Further up the road is Delaware. Rutherford B. Hayes, nineteenth President of the United States was born here. There is a monument that marks his place of birth.

From Delaware the route picks up U.S. 42 to State 95 into Marion. Named after Gen. Francis Marion, the "Swamp Fox" of the American Revolution, the city is most noted for two things; popcorn and Warren G. Harding. The former fought its way to the top in frying pans across the nation while the latter went from State Senator through the political line and finally popped into the White House as our twenty-ninth president.

The Harding Home and Museum is the house he built during his courtship and was the scene of his famous 1920 "Front Porch" campaign.

Near the junction at Upper Sandusky is the Wyandot Mission Church.

Approximate mileage: 100.

Best times for touring: April through October.

Terrain: Local highways; some hills, but no big ones.

Traffic: Light.

Historical points of interest: Columbus, Ohio State University, President Hayes' birthplace, home of President Harding, Methodist Mission, Findlay.

To Toledo

To Akron

To Lima

To Mansfield

To Springfield

HULL OLD TRAIL MONUMENT

Tiffin

Findlay

THE WYANDOT MISSION

Upper Sandusky

Bucyrus

Galion

Kenton

HARDING HOME

Marion

Mt. Gilead

HARDING MEMORIAL

Delaware Lake

Delaware

HAYES MONUMENT

Marysville

PERKINS OBSERVATORY

Hoover Res.

OHIO ST. UNIV.

COLUMBUS

London

© The H.M. Gousha Co.

To Cincinnati

Established in 1816, it was the first Methodist Mission in Ohio. Indian and pioneer artifacts are on display at the Wyandot County Historical Society.

Follow the map through the gentle hills to Findlay. In the 1850's this town was the site of the "Grapevine Telegraph" and Underground Railroad, which piloted runaway slaves to safety. The flowing Blanchard River nearby inspired Tell Taylor to write the classic ballad, "Down by the Old Mill Stream." End your Ohio excursion with a visit to the Hull Old Trail Monument.

Rolling Ride to the "Old Swimmin' Hole"

The rolling roads of Indiana combine with an art colony and historical highlights to make this 145 mile Hoosier holiday a mighty fine cycling time. And you can end your tour sitting by "The Old Swimmin' Hole" that James Whitcomb Riley immortalized.

The tour begins at Spring Mill State Park, off State Route 60. There are overnight camping facilities here. Also on the grounds is a restoration of Spring Mill Village which was founded about 1815. You can buy meal ground by the old mill housed in the restored two story stone building. In contrast to the lapping sounds of the old water wheel is a monument to a man who lived with the thunder of space age rockets. Virgil I. Grissom, who was raised in nearby Mitchell, was killed in a flash fire on a simulation of one of the Apollo flights. The second American in space, a memorial now honors Grissom at the park.

The route follows State 37 through Mitchell to Bedford, famous as the stone capital of the U.S. You will see limestone quarries as you pedal into town. Parts of the Empire State Building, Chicago Museum of Fine Arts and other famous structures came from the Bedford pits.

Head east via State 58 to State 135. North, past the Hoosier National Forest, you'll head into Brown County State Park. The largest park in the state, it has more than 15,000 acres of hilly drives, a wildlife sanctuary, exhibits of Indiana's once plentiful animals, such as elk, bear and buffalo. From an observation tower atop Weed Patch Hill you can peruse the countryside. Accommodations during the summer are available at a 40-room, cabin-style state park operation. Make reservations.

Just up the road a piece is Nashville. You're not going to hear a lot of guitar finger-pickin' in *this* Nashville but what your ears miss your eyes will make up

Approximate mileage: 145.

Best times for touring: April through October.

Terrain: Somewhat hilly.

Traffic: Some tourist traffic in the fall but they are usually sightseeing and are in no hurry.

Historical points of interest: James Whitcomb Riley birthplace, Nashville, Grissom Memorial at Mitchell.

for. This is art country. Famous artists and craftsmen have work on display. The Brown County Art Gallery Association is one of the oldest and most respected art centers in the midwest. At Valley View Farm a couple of miles out of town off State Route 46 there is a campground in case you want to bed down and take a few days to soak up more artistic atmosphere.

Take State 46 through Columbus, then grab State 9 heading north to Greenfield. Here is the Hoosier homeland of James Whitcomb Riley, popular Indiana poet who was born and raised here. The restored home where he grew up is open to the public.

To end your Indiana tour have a picnic at Riley Memorial Park and sit by the poet's "Old Swimmin' Hole."

Three Short Tours on Chicago's Lakefront

Bike riding along the shore of Lake Michigan can be delightful diversion for an hour or a full day. You can bite off any length tour that suits your family and your endurance. All start near Ohio St.

Riding along Lake Shore Drive is easy; a wide walkway on the ocean side of the roadway lets you cruise along without being trapped by auto traffic. Keep an eye on pedestrians, though.

A north loop of six miles can be made along the lakefront up into Lincoln Park, with a detour along Michigan Ave. if you are willing to put up with busy city traffic to see the best of Chicago's shopping districts. At Chicago and Michigan Avenues is the famous Old Water Tower that survived the 1871 fire.

The ride north toward the park is very scenic, with views of both the lakeshore activities and the towering buildings of downtown (the tallest of all in this northern area is the John Hancock Center, which you pass on the return ride down Michigan Ave).

Lincoln Park is a treasure trove. There are fine picnic areas, a zoo, animal farm, lagoons and the Academy of Sciences. Take them as time allows, and then return to the lakefront via the tunnel or pedestrian walk.

A short five mile trip south of Ohio Street will take you past Grant Park with its Art Institute and Buckingham Fountain, and down to the Museum of Natural History and Shedd Aquarium, two excellent places to explore on foot. (Bike theft can be a problem here, so be sure to lock your bikes securely to a fence or tree, preferably within clear view of a concessionaire or guard.)

The third and by far the longest ride is an additional 14 miles to Jackson Park, home of the Museum of Science and Industry, one of Chicago's top attractions, then off to the east to Washington Park, and back to the lakefront.

Approximate mileage: 6, North Loop; 5, Grant Park; add. 14, Jackson Park.

Best times for touring: Spring through fall; strong winds off the lake.

Terrain: Generally flat, with only a few grades. Wide walkway.

Traffic: Walkway o.k., but city streets are congested.

Points of interest: Water Tower, Lincoln Park Museums, Museum of Natural History, Museum of Science and Industry.

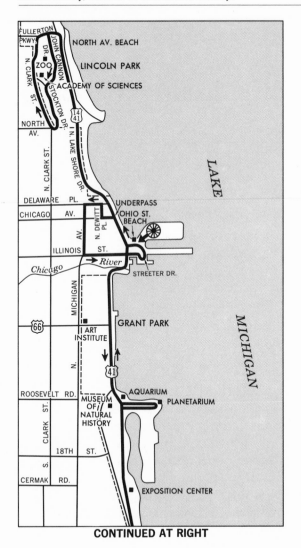

CONTINUED AT RIGHT

CONTINUED FROM LEFT

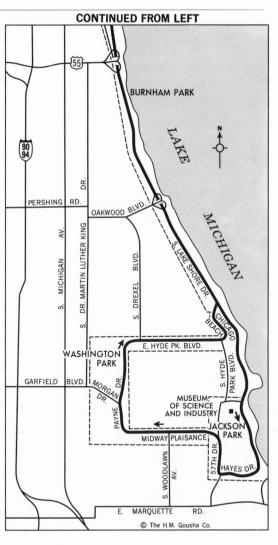

© The H.M. Gousha Co.

Recycle the Lincoln-Douglas Debate Scene

Three states combine to blend a hardy mixture of history and easy cycling on this 160-mile tour through the land where Lincoln and Douglas held their famous debate.

The tour begins at Quincy, accessible via U.S. 24. Motels are available and there is camping near Sid Simpson State Park. Many monuments and statues dot the town, commemorating the four governors of Illinois, four Union Army generals and one Confederate general that made the city their home. The statue that draws the most people concerns a couple of fellows running for the U.S. Senate back in 1858. In Washington Park Abraham Lincoln and Stephen A. Douglas had a famous duel of words that helped launch Lincoln on to political greatness. The Quincy Historic Museum contains memorabilia from this city. Another claim to fame of the area is the Reverend John Patrick Kerr, the first black priest in the United States.

Cross the Mississippi River and head north on U.S. 61 through La Grange (camping near here) to Keokuk. Founded in 1820 this city was named for a Sauk Indian chief. Mark Twain worked here for awhile as a printer. There is a campground at Chatfield Park three miles west.

The route picks up U.S. 61 north to Ft. Madison. About two miles out of Ft. Madison you will be able to find a campsite at Rodeo Park.

Out of town you will again cross the mighty Mississippi, this time paying a toll. The tour takes State 96 south to Nauvoo, a town drenched in history. Originally called Commerce, the name was changed to Nauvoo in 1839 when Joseph Smith, the prophet of the Mormons led his people to the tiny village. The Mormons built the town from almost nothing to the largest city in Illinois. Having been driven out of Missouri, the religious group hoped to make a permanent settlement in Illi-

Approximate mileage: 160.

Best times for touring: April through October.

Terrain: Mostly flat over good paved roads.

Traffic: Moderate.

Historical points of interest: Lincoln-Douglas Debate site at Quincy, Nauvoo, Carthage jail.

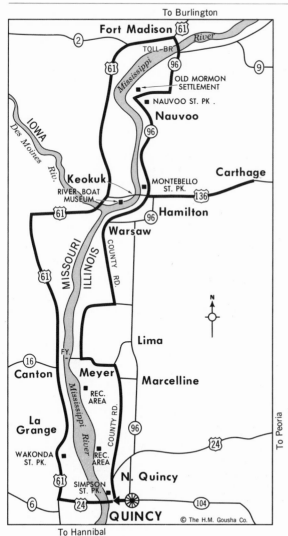

nois. In 1841, construction began on a great temple.

But misfortune continued to haunt Smith and his followers. A schism in the church and threat of Mormon political power led to riots and persecution of the group. The violence culminated with the murder of Smith and his brother at the jail in Carthage. Brigham Young became leader of the Nauvoo Mormons and led them to their permanent home in Utah.

The next group to try for a home here was the Icarians, a band of French who believed in communal living. The utopian colony failed but the influence of the group fostered the "Wedding of Wine and Cheese," a festival held every year the weekend before Labor Day. There are accommodations.

The tour continues down State Route 96 to U.S. 136 and heads east to Carthage for a first hand look at the jail where Joseph Smith and his brother were held. Recycle yourself back to the main route and follow the route south back to the departure point in Quincy.

Down the Abandoned Track from Elroy to Sparta

Wisconsin's Elroy-Sparta State Trail is a quiet 30-mile ride through a tree-clad land that once roared with the sounds of the railroad.

Now the once noisy trail is silent; no motor vehicles are allowed to disturb the solitude of the rocky hills and colorful wildflowers. The route follows the abandoned railroad from Elroy through a series of three tunnels to the town of Sparta.

The starting point at Elroy can be reached by State Routes 80 and 71.

The community of Elroy has a city park, with a small man-made lake, swimming pool, camping and hotel accommodations, including the historic 28-room Elroy Hotel. Also available are bike rentals, here and at Kendall, Wilton, Norwalk and Sparta.

As you pedal out of Elroy you will be heading into land that is surrounded by 100 years of railroad history. The Chicago & Northwestern Railroad completed the line in fall of 1873. The 32-mile stretch of old railroad is unique because three large tunnels were built between Sparta and Elroy. (Hopefully your cycle is equipped with a light.)

In 1965 the Northwestern Railroad ceased operation of the line and the right-of-way was sold to the Wisconsin Conservation Department. The department developed the biking and hiking trail and opened it to the public in 1966.

The first landmark you will reach is the town of Kendall. The last railroad depot on the line is being renovated here to provide picnic and restroom facilities for the cyclists and hikers. Also here is a beautiful park with room for overnight camping, picnic areas, fireplaces and a shelter house.

Between Kendall and the next town of Wilton you will pass through tunnel number one. It's 1,680 feet long and it is suggested that you turn on your lights and walk your bike to the other end.

About five miles past this tunnel is Wilton. Another hospitable town, it

Approximate mileage: 30 miles, one way.

Best time for touring: In the spring for the trees and wildflowers and in the fall for the magnificent color.

Terrain: Compacted fine gravel, minimal grades.

Traffic: None. No automobiles allowed.

Historical points of interest: Old train route with three tunnels; Sparta.

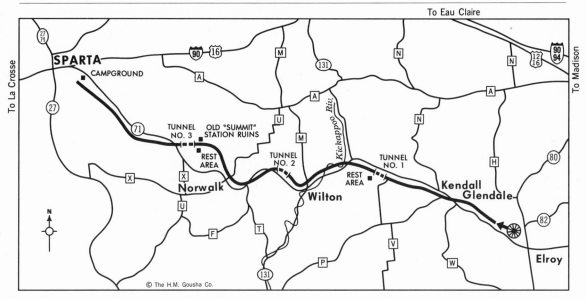

boasts one of the most beautiful park and recreational centers in western Wisconsin. There are overnight camping facilities, a picnic area and even a stocked trout pond.

Just a couple of miles out of Wilton is the second tunnel. It's about the same length as the first and again it's advisable to walk through.

Norwalk is the next town on the route. Here on October 15th, 1902, the Old '97 Flyer collided nearly head-on with a freight train. The collision caused extensive property damage and numerous injuries but no deaths.

The largest tunnel which lies a few miles out of Norwalk took three years to build.

Outside of Norwalk, before entering the last tunnel, there is a turnoff for Ridgeville. Here, atop a ridge that offers a spectacular view of the distant valleys, is the Farmhouse Hostel.

The next adventure is the big tunnel, over 3,810 long. It is the last landmark before Sparta.

Circus History on Baraboo Round Robin

Circus history, Fort Winnebago, traces of the fur trading days are all on the route that laces around through scenic Wisconsin countryside.

You won't run into problems on this route. The entire tour winds through easy, rolling countryside. Much of the northern part of the loop is along the Wisconsin River through Pine Island Refuge.

Start at Baraboo and immediately head for 430 Water St. and the Circus World Museum. At this original home of Ringling Bros. you can enjoy a live performance, see old parade wagons and other circus relics. Part of the Historical Society of Wisconsin, the 15 colorful acres are open mid-May through mid-September from 9 a.m. to 5:30 p.m. and admission is charged.

To really begin the tour, get on your bike and strike out down Hwy. W, which is a designated bikeway. Wisconsin dairy lands will stretch out around you for miles as you ride along Rowley Creek. At a wide fork in the road, choose the left road and pick up Hwy. 33 into Portage.

An optional side trip you might like to take is the Cascade Mt. Ski Area, 4 miles south of Portage.

Portage is the point between the Fox and Wisconsin Rivers where early French fur traders carried their goods between waterways. Later the Old Ship Canal was dug to provide portage, giving the town its name. Fort Winnebago was erected on the site before the town developed and there are remains of several historic points of interest.

The Old Indian Agency House, built in 1832, is on Agency Rd. off State 33. This restored home of an Indian agent contains period furnishings and is open May-October, 9 a.m. to 5 p.m. and the rest of the year by appointment.

One mile east of town on State 33 you'll find a log cabin survivor of Fort Winnebago—quarters for the medical officers stationed at the post. There is

Approx. mileage: 40, loop trip; 10 extra to Devil's Lake State Park.

Best times for touring: Early summer in June, after Labor Day.

Terrain: Level to gently rolling; one slight hill north of Baraboo; side trip hilly.

Traffic: Summer traffic heavy around Portage.

Historical points of interest: Circus World Museum, Fort Winnebago Surgeons' Quarters, Indian Agency House, Sauk County Museum.

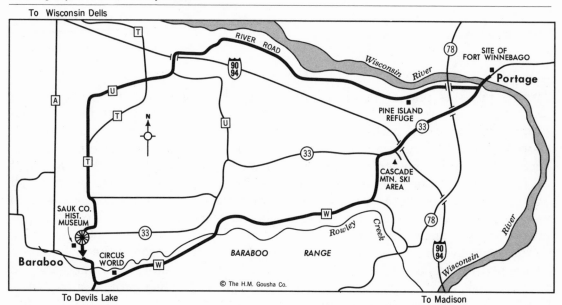

To Wisconsin Dells

To Devils Lake

To Madison

also a garrison school.

Ride northwest from Portage along the Wisconsin River on River Road. The trip here is especially delightful because you ride through the Pine Island refuge. It is really quite wild, with geese, ducks, foxes, lots of deer and a bountiful display of plant life.

Cross over Int. 90-94 and join Hwy. U. Pick up Hwy. T just north of Baraboo, where you'll encounter a slight hill.

Back in Baraboo you may want to get some historical background of the area. The Sauk County Historical Museum is at 531 4th Ave. and displays Indian artifacts, Civil War memorabilia as well as geological information of the unusual glacial and preglacial surrounding terrain.

The short side trip to Devil's Lake State Park will give you a fascinating insight into the unusual remnants of an old range of mountains.

Milwaukee: Parks, Lake Michigan and History

This is rated as one of the best city tours in the entire country. It passes through many scenic parks, skirts the shore of Lake Michigan and gives cyclists a very thorough look at the city of Milwaukee from one end to the other. It makes good use of the extensive parkway network, and even takes in some of the open countryside.

The city's history goes back to the time when the Indians called it Mahn-a-waukee Seepe, "gathering place by the river." Several tribes lived in the area, most notably the Potawatomi. A French trading post was founded by Solomon Juneau in 1818. The city began developing in the 1830's, with Juneau playing a prominent role as intepreter and peacemaker between the whites and the Indians. (Early on the bike tour, you pass through Juneau Park, named after this most important of Milwaukee's early settlers.)

In the late 1830's began the immigration of Irish, Yankees, Poles and particularly Germans who were to play so great a role in the political and social development of Milwaukee. The growth of the city continued steadily over the next century, but Milwaukee managed to hold onto a good part of its small town flavor until a post World War II boom propelled it into one of the major commercial centers of the Great Lakes.

As you cycle through the town, you'll see a good mixture of old and new, the German and Polish heritage mixed with the modern developments that threaten to overpower the older traditions.

No description of a Milwaukee tour would be complete without a mention of the county zoo, one of the finest in the country. It's not right on the route, but it is only a few blocks' detour from the path as it crosses the city's west side. If you have the time for a short stop, be sure to spend an hour or two wandering through the grounds (it's free if you arrive before 11 a.m.).

If you are carrying a picnic lunch

Approximate mileage: 64.

Best times for tourings: May to October.

Terrain: Generally flat, with a few mild climbs.

Traffic: It can be heavy anywhere in the city; caution is urged on all city streets, especially those in the downtown area.

Historical points of interest: Greek Orthodox Church, Juneau Park.

there are ample opportunities to enjoy it in one of the major parks traversed by the bikeway. If you'd rather sit in a restaurant and be served, again no problem since the route stays in populated areas for the most part. Whitnall Park near the southern end of the bike ride is the largest park in the city; if you're looking for a detour in this very scenic area, ride over to the Boerner Botanical Gardens; no charge for admission.

At the intersection of 92nd St. and Grantosa, watch for the Greek Orthodox Church (it fronts on Congress Street); the design by Frank Lloyd Wright gives it special prominence in the city's architecture.

Milwaukee to Madison on Wisconsin's Bikeway

This is a long ride across Wisconsin's fabled dairylands, linking the Milwaukee commercial center with the state capital at Madison. Starting at the Red Barn Hostel in Milwaukee, the southern part of the route passes over some of the Wisconsin Bikeway (see pages 126 and 134 for other tours on the Bikeway). It generally follows lightly traveled county and town roads. The only city actually transited is Waukesha, but you will also find traffic in the eastern part of Madison.

This is a favorite two-day trip with the Wisconsin AYH. If you want to join one of their trips, or get more information about the route, write to Box 233, Hales Corners, Wisconsin 53130. Accommodations and picnic grounds are plentiful along the route.

The southern unit of Kettle Moraine State Forest is open to exploration at several points. It is generally forested land with many camping and picnicking facilities. Whitewater Lake at the southern tip of the Forest is easily reachable from the alternate bike route through Delavan.

If you have a chocolate freak in the bicycling party, be sure to allow time for a stop at the Nestle plant in Burlington. By phoning ahead for reservations (763-9111) you can take a tour of the candy plant on most weekdays.

All around Lake Geneva is a very extensive and popular resort area, which is likely to be crowded during the vacation months, particularly on weekends. Big Foot Beach State Park is a popular stop.

One of the most historic spots on the loop is the Milton House Museum, open daily through the summer months. A hexagonal structure, it was built in 1844.

Waukesha was settled in the 1830's and the Waukesha County Historical Museum in the Courthouse is a good place to go for more information about the entire area.

Approximate mileage: 200.

Best times for touring: May to October.

Terrain: Mostly flat.

Traffic: Not too crowded, except in Waukesha, roads near Madison, and intersections with state and U.S. highways.

Historical points of interest: Dairy country, Milton House Museum, Waukesha History Museum.

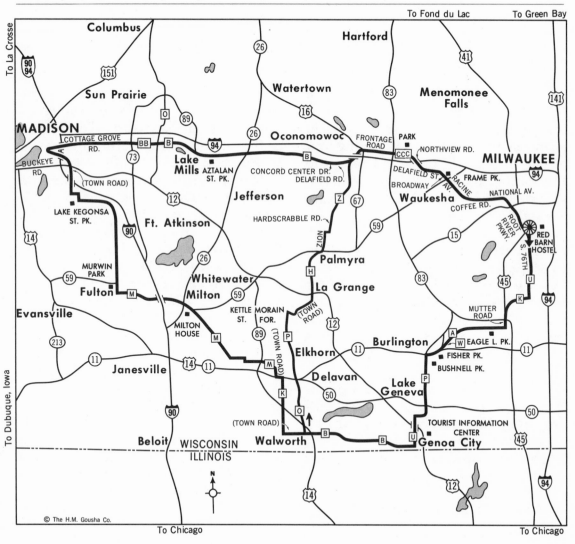

Smooth, Easy Jaunt Through the Dairyland

This one-way route is a piece out of Wisconsin's extensive bike trail system. It's not a difficult ride and its crescent shape enables you to break off the tour at one of several points and return to the starting point, cycle into Madison or Janesville, or even join the Milwaukee ride (see page 132).

South of Sauk City, the starting point, the route follows the Wisconsin River to Mazomanie on a level road. At Black Earth, you take Highway F toward Blue Mounds, an attractive hilly area inhabited mainly by Norwegian and Swiss-Americans, whose ancestors sought an area similar to the lands they left behind.

At the top of the hill is Blue Mounds State Park, near an area of rock outcroppings and lovely views. Nearby Lost River Cave and Cave of the Mounds are open to the public during summer months, and both charge fees.

New Glarus may be the cheese capital of the nation, and you can see how Swiss cheese is made, sample the good food, and have your choice of some excellent handcrafts. To the east is the famous dairy farm country of Dayton and Attica.

The stretch between Evansville and Milton is gently rolling country, until you hit the Rock Prairie right at Milton. This is perfectly flat cropland. Around Rock River you'll find a number of historic homes and antique shops, and in the city of Milton is the historic hexagonal Milton House Museum which dates back to 1844.

Around Walworth is an abundance of recreational opportunities—resorts on Lake Geneva and Delavan Lake, camping and picnicking at Big Foot Beach State Park.

At Walworth, you're riding a Milwaukee-Madison run (page 132) so you have a choice of continuing along this path to Milwaukee, riding back to Milton and into Madison, or retracing this tour.

Approximate mileage: 75.

Best times for touring: Spring through fall, approximately May to October.

Terrain: Generally flat, with some climbs near Blue Mounds.

Traffic: Light, except for intersections with state routes.

Historical points of interest: Milton House Museum, area around Rock River.

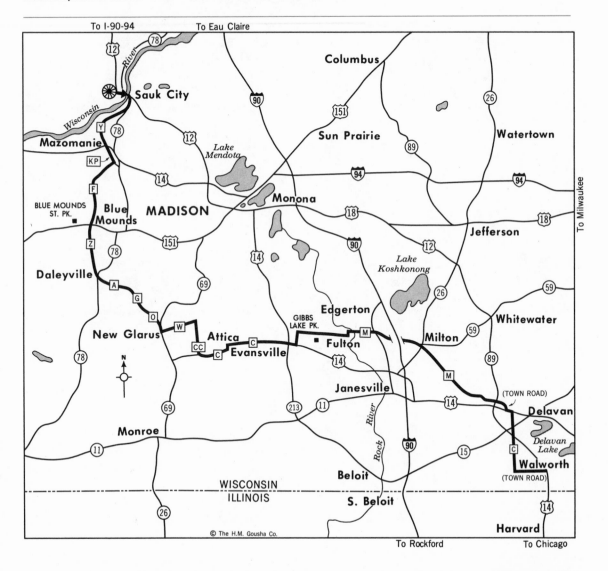

Plains-Rockies

St. Joseph and the Pony Express Riders

A roller coasterlike ride with long slopes and tight curves makes this tour through the heart of St. Joseph, Missouri an exciting cycle adventure.

Over a century ago St. Joseph was one of the authentic frontier towns. It was a rendezvous of Jesse James, the notorious outlaw who roamed over much of this area. The hard riding boys of the Pony Express also got their start in this Missouri city.

The tour begins at Hyde Park, which can be reached via U.S. 59 to Alabama St. from the west or off U.S. 36 from the east.

Leave the park on the Southwest Parkway and follow the route out to Northwest Parkway, which will take you to Krug Park.

Along the way, off Messanie Street is the Jesse James home. In this one-story frame cottage the infamous outlaw lived quietly as "Mr. Howard" until he was killed there April 3, 1882 by a former associate. Krug Park has picnic grounds and is an excellent spot for lunch under the trees before embarking on the route back. The park also has the Krug Park Bowl, which seats over 20,000 persons and is the site for many public music and dramatic functions. You might want to check ahead so you could time your ride to catch a performance.

From Krug Park take the Northwest Parkway to Lovers Lane and head south. The Lane got its romantic title from a poem by Eugene Field, entitled appropriately, "Lover's Lane, Saint Jo." It seems the poet was prevented from marrying the girl of his fancy, Julia Comstock, so while pining away in London he penned the love ballad.

From here, take Maple Leaf Parkway off Lovers Lane to 4th St. and head south to Francis. Just off Francis on 914 Penn St. is the Pony Express Stables Museum. On the site of the starting point for the Express riders the old stables were rebuilt in 1886. Open from

Approximate mileage: 15, round trip.

Best times for touring: Any season.

Terrain: Narrow parkway with a lot of curves, climbs and long coasts.

Traffic: Caution is advised where downtown traffic is a problem.

Historical points of interest: Pony Express Museum.

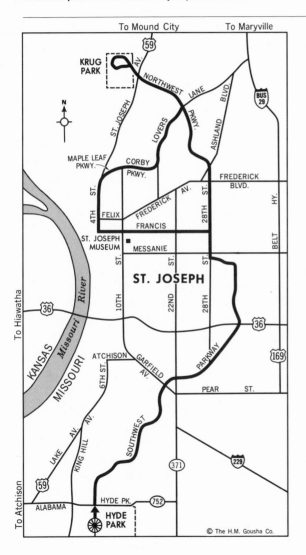

May to mid-September, displays trace the wild history of the Pony Express.

Mail service was inaugurated at 5 p.m. on the afternoon of April 3, 1860. "Little Jonnie" Frey mounted his pony and, while hundreds cheered, he dashed off on the first lap of the 1,975-mile trip to California. The express maintained a schedule of about ten days for each trip and hired such famed riders as "Buffalo Bill" Cody, "Pony" Bob Haslem and Jack Slade to insure the company's reputation for fast delivery. The Express lasted a dusty, hoof-thomping 16 months before giving way to the cleaner, more efficient telegraph.

The tour continues down Francis Street back to the Southwest Parkway. From here it's a topsy turvy ride through the tight curves, long hills and nice coasts. Watch out for the traffic as there isn't much space. The tour ends at the beginning, Hyde Park. There are picnic facilities here, so you might relax and have something to eat before the drive home.

From Truman Library to Lexington Battlefield

This Missouri tour takes the cyclist through quiet farmland to the historic battlefield of Lexington where cannons once thundered the sounds of civil war.

The departure point for the tour is the county courthouse in Independence. Daniel Boone is credited with being the first white man to visit the site of this Missouri city. Permanent settlers didn't arrive until 1825 when the Indian title was relinquished to the United States.

Before starting the tour visit the Harry S. Truman Library. (Also, see page 142.)

Another worthwhile stop is at the auditorium of the Reorganized Church of Latter Day Saints, which head-quarters here. In 1831, Joseph Smith, prophet of the Mormon Church, came to Independence and proclaimed it the promised land.

This historic tour takes Truman Road which becomes County Road FF out of Independence. For the next twenty miles you'll cruise along quiet farmland roads, turning on to State 224 to Lexington.

On the northern edge of Lexington on Sixteenth St. is College Park, site of the first Masonic College in the world. The college was moved to Lexington in 1846 and closed in 1859. Within the park is the open-sided Memorial Building which houses memorial plaques, a map of the Lexington battlefield and pictures of historic scenes. Stay on Sixteenth St. a short distance from the memorial, and you will find the marker and gates of the Lexington battlefield, now an 80-acre Confederate Memorial Park.

Here is some historical background to help you understand the park. The Battle of Lexington was fought in September, 1861, between General Sterling Price's Confederate troops and Colonel James A. Mulligan's Union forces.

General Price placed his troops on three sides of the Union entrenchment

Approximate mileage: 35, one way.

Best time for touring: Spring or fall.

Terrain: Some long hills near Independence; mostly back country roads.

Traffic: Light, except in Independence.

Historical points of interest: Harry S. Truman Library, Mormon Auditorium, Lexington Battlefield Park.

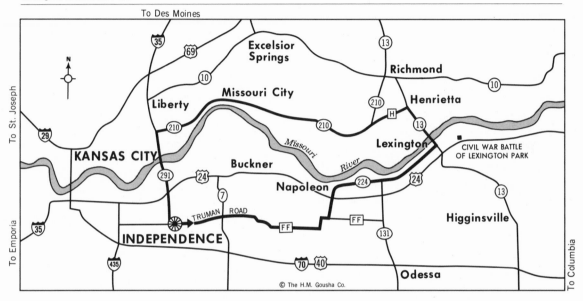

on this strategic Missouri River port and demanded surrender. Colonel Mulligan refused. The Union held out for three days before being forced to surrender.

The ante bellum Anderson House around which the battle was fought now has a museum on the second and third floors with pictures, guns, swords and other relics from the 1860's. The Lexington courthouse has a remarkable cannonball on top of a column.

There are two reasonably priced restaurants in Lexington and a motel south on State 13.

The tour can be doubled by taking the same route back to Independence or by an alternate path on the other side of the Missouri River. Take State 13 over the river and follow the tour back to Independence. Expect fairly heavy traffic. Because of frequent south or west winds, this tour is easier going than returning.

Arrow Rock Escape on the Wide Missouri

Escape from the city and take a long trek to a rewarding destination on this tour through the Missouri countryside to Arrow Rock on the Missouri River.

The starting point for the ride is Independence, Missouri, at State 7 and County Road FF. Before heading out, stop to see the Harry S. Truman Library that houses the late President's library-office and also contains artifacts from his life.

The tour now turns away from the city on county route FF heading east. Tranquility becomes a reality as you cruise along this back country road.

State 131 cuts across FF about 15 miles out of Independence. A few miles past this junction County Route O will also intersect FF. Make a left here for a short loop trip to historic Lexington Battlefield.

Since the next town is 25 miles away you may want to stay the night in Lexington and leisurely take in the history of the area.

On the northern edge of Lexington at Sixteenth St. is a landscaped area on the Missouri River bluff. Within this city-owned park is the open-sided Memorial Building, housing memorial plaques and maps of the Lexington Battlefield. Further down Sixteenth are the marker and gates of the battlefield. In September, 1861, General Sterling Price's Confederate troops engaged Colonel James A. Mulligan's Union forces in an important conflict.

Prior to the battle, Lexington, like other Missouri River posts, was held by the Union to prevent the northern and southern branches of the Confederacy from joining. After a bloody three-day siege the Union was forced to surrender.

The Anderson House around which the battle was fought is now a historical landmark. During the battle this three-story, red brick structure was occupied by the Union as a hospital.

To get back on the route take State

Approximate mileage: 75, one way; 95 with loop trip.

Best times for touring: Spring and fall.

Terrain: Mostly backroads through farmland.

Traffic: Light, except in Independence, other towns.

Historical points of interest: Arrow Rock State Park, Lexington Confederate Memorial Park, Truman Library.

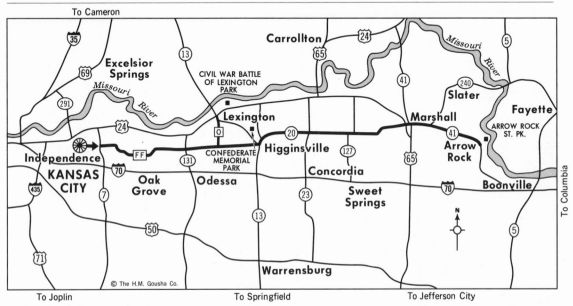

13 out of Lexington about seven miles to State 20 and head east.

From here it's straight road with only an occasional small town for twenty miles. Marshall has a good dining room at the Inn and a motel if you're not ready for the last 15 or so miles to Arrow Rock.

Arrow Rock, an authentic old river town, is a nice place to end a journey. At the Old Tavern in Arrow Rock Park you can get some old-fashioned country food. Missouri ham is a real treat. Arrow Park has some historical tidbits as tasty as the countrified cuisine. According to legend the area derived its name from a contest for a fair Indian maiden. The winner shot his arrow so far it lodged in the bluff.

Arrow Rock Park has good overnight camping facilities. On this tour, the wind is usually from the west, so expect the return trip to Independence to be a little tougher.

Ride to the Scene of John Brown's Raid

John Brown, famed abolitionist, fought a battle that cost the lives of five of his men at Osawatomie, the destination of this 32 mile Kansas tour.

Johnson County Airport is a good starting place. Follow the route over to U.S. 169. For a couple of miles near Spring Hill, take extra care as the traffic is high speed and the road narrow.

Paola has an interesting town square and court house. There is a pleasant picnic facility just out of Osawatomie.

Osawatomie is said to have been named for the two Indian tribes living in the vicinity, the Osage and the Potawatomi. In 1856 the little town became a battleground. John Brown, who later became famous for his raid on Harpers Ferry in 1859, led a group of men to Osawatomie to protect the town from terrorists. About 400 pro-slavery men, under Gen. John W. Reid, were moving to burn the city. Brown and fifteen men rushed to the vicinity to recruit men. Both parties arrived at about the same time. Brown and his band that now numbered 30 camped just west of the Adair homestead and Reid camped north of the town. On the morning of August 30, 1856, Reid advanced, and the defenders opened fire. Many of Reid's men fell, but when the pro-slavery men brought up the cannons Brown and his men were forced to retreat. Reid's losses were heavy, 70 men were killed or wounded. Five of Brown's men were killed. The town was leveled by fire as the pro-slavery men completed their mission.

Other reports of the action differ greatly as to the scale of the battle. A report by Col F. J. Snyder, of Reid's forces, said, "The engagement didn't last three hours as is generally thought; and to call it a battle is ludicrous, I knew nothing of the strength or losses of the John Brown forces, but we had a few wounded and none killed."

Judge James Hale, a lieutenant with the pro-slavery party, claims that on

Approx. mileage: 32, one way.

Best times for touring: Fall or cool summer days.

Terrain: High speed highways over flat lands.

Traffic: Moderate, one bad spot two miles north of Spring Hill.

Historical points of interest: John Brown's cabin and Old Stone Church in Osawatomie; Paola city square.

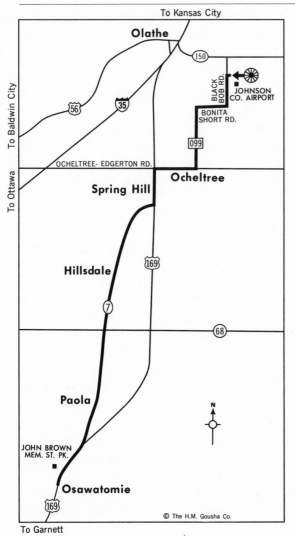

To Kansas City

Olathe

150

BLACK BOB RD.

JOHNSON CO. AIRPORT

BONITA SHORT RD.

56

35

099

OCHELTREE- EDGERTON RD.

Ocheltree

Spring Hill

Hillsdale

169

7

68

Paola

N

JOHN BROWN MEM. ST. PK.

Osawatomie

169

© The H.M. Gousha Co.

To Baldwin City

To Ottawa

To Garnett

August 30, 1856, Reid's troops advanced and encountered three of John Brown's pickets. They were shot in a quick skirmish. Hale agrees that none of Reid's men were killed and only a few wounded.

Well, whatever happened it helped make John Brown a Civil War figure. Brown was hanged in 1859 after Gen. Robert E. Lee captured him in an attempt to sieze and control the U.S. arsenal at Harpers Ferry (see page 66.) In the west part of town is the John Brown Memorial Park, which contains a life-size statue of the abolitionist and the log cabin he used. Open Tuesday through Sunday. Free. Another point of interest in Osawatomie is the restored Original Land Office on Lincoln Avenue.

Lolo Trail – Pathway for Lewis and Clark

Beautiful and treacherous mountains, trout filled streams and tall trees of the Clearwater National Forest are the gateways to the Lewis and Clark trail through parts of Montana and Idaho. You can cycle along the highway, U.S. 12, that parallels the explorers' path for 143 miles along the Indians' Lolo Trail.

Early in your expedition you will stop at the campsites of these first white men to explore and record their impressions of the great Northwest and Idaho's Nez Perce Indians.

This tour is great for the modern day adventurer as civilization is a rare commodity along the route. Bring equipment for minor repairs on your bike as there are no towns with services. There is also a 66 mile stretch with no stores, so be prepared to carry some grub. Another item which should prove handy is a sleeping bag; campgrounds are more abundant out here than motels. Mittens for the higher al-titudes are also a good idea.

Missoula, Montana, home of the University of Montana, is the starting point of the trip. Pick up U.S. 12 at Lolo for the pull up to Lolo Pass. Lolo Hot Springs are located near the pass and the visitors' center. Lewis' and Clark's journey took them to the same spot and they enjoyed the hot baths provided by the springs. When the Indian guides with their party jumped from the hot springs into the icy cold water of Lolo Creek, the explorers were amused, recording this incident in their journals.

Pass DeVoto Grove Recreation Center before you come to Powell. This is a good place to garner a few groceries to cook at one of the many campsites along the route.

Edging the Selway-Bitterroot Wilderness Area, you now cycle along for miles with barely an indication of civilization. A couple of interesting rest stops as you ride along the Lochsa

Approximate mileage: 143.

Best times for touring: Summer.

Terrain: Gradual uphill climb until the steep grade leading to the summit.

Traffic: No problem; good shoulders and polite motorists.

Historical points of interest: Lewis and Clark expedition campsites, Nez Perce Indian lands.

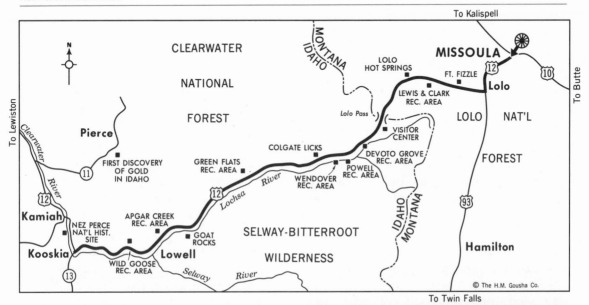

River are Colgate Licks and Goat Rocks. Lowell is another tiny settlement.

Narrow, deep canyons cradle a variety of plant life—pine, fir, cedar, larch and spruce line the sparkling trout and salmon streams. Wild life, such as elk, moose, mountain goat and bears abound in the area. In 1805 the Lewis and Clark expedition stumbled half starved out of these treacherous mountains into what is now Kooskia, the end, also, of your ride.

Wildlife Odyssey to Indian Territory

Lakes and buffalo highlight this 220 mile loop tour from Missoula out through the wide open territory of Montana.

Way back in the days of Lewis and Clark, Missoula was an Indian trading and trail crossroads and bears that distinction to this day. Later the site attracted not only Indians but explorers, hunting and trading parties. Today farmers, manufacturers and merchants abound in the city. Before leaving the city visit the University of Montana and the Aerial Fire Depot, with tours of parachute lofts, fire control exhibits and information on recreational facilities in the 16 national forests in the area. Another Missoula attraction are the historic Paxson paintings at the county courthouse.

The tour takes State 200 out of the town east through Potomac to State Route 209 and heads north to Seeley Lake. Camp and picnic grounds are available here.

Paralleling the Swan River you ride for miles through the beautiful river valley to Condon and Woodward.

From this town you get a good view of Flathead Lake, the largest freshwater body of water west of the Great Lakes.

Continue on, taking State 35 south along the mammoth lake. Camping, fishing, hunting and a wide variety of other outdoor activities are available at Montana's biggest water playground.

Past the lake the tour takes U.S. 93 south through Pablo and Ronan to the Ninepipe National Wildlife Refuge. Birds flock to this natural haven and present a colorful feathery display for bird fanciers.

Just down the road is the National Bison Range, the home of an enormous herd of shaggy animals known to most as buffalo, along with elk, pronghorns, whitetail and mule deer.

St. Ignatius Mission, established in 1854 for the Flathead Indians is nearby. Some consider the mission to be among

Approximate mileage: 220.

Best times for touring: May through September.

Terrain: Varied, from gradual to steep grades.

Traffic: Can be a problem, as many summer homes are along the route.

Historical points of interest: Ninepipe National Wildlife Refuge, St. Ignatius, Montana National Bison Range.

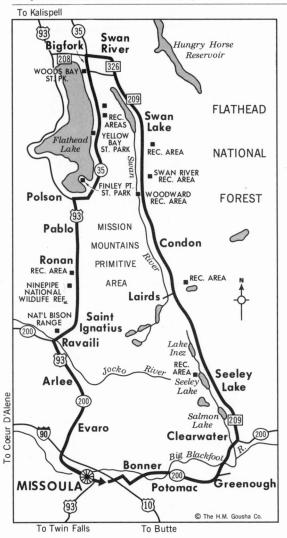

the world's most beautiful.

The route picks up State Route 200 through Evaro and heads back to the departure point at Missoula. (See also the Montana tour on page 146.)

Rugged Mountaineering in Spectacular Montana

Hundreds of miles of sensational mountain scenery in Montana is the reward of this grueling haul for rugged cyclists. There are motels in the main towns but other nights plan on reaching a campground before sundown.

The tour begins at Kalispell off U.S. 93. This city is the Christmas tree capital of the Flathead Valley, shipping out over one and one-half million trees annually. Visit the Flathead Historical Society Museum which contains a grave of an aboriginal Indian.

The route follows Flathead Lake. There is camping at Flathead Lake State Park, along with swimming and fishing.

South of here is the Pablo National Wildlife Refuge, where you can see over 185 species of birds, then the town of Ronan and Ninepipe Wildlife Refuge. Also near here is the National Bison Range where three to five hundred of the shaggy beasts roam.

The tour continues south to the junction of U.S. 10. From here you can take a 20-mile sidetrip to Missoula. Highlights include a visit to the University of Montana and Fort Missoula.

Back on the main route you will pass the Quartz and Cascade Recreational areas. Both are good places to bed down for the night.

At the junction of State Route 28 you can shorten the loop many miles by heading north to Flathead Lake.

For the adventurous who are continuing, the tour picks up State 200 through the green hills of Lolo National Forest. Camping and picnic sites abound in the many recreational spots.

Through Thompson Falls follow the map to Noxon Rapids Dam which is an interesting stopping point. Further north near Troy is the American Wildlife Museum; and in Libby look in at the fish hatchery.

Wind your way back through the mountains, lakes and streams to Kalispell and the end of your long Montana adventure.

Approximate mileage: 498.

Best times for touring: June through September.

Terrain: Hilly, over good secondary roads.

Traffic: Moderate.

Historical points of interest: American Wildlife Museum, National Bison Range, University of Montana, Fort Missoula.

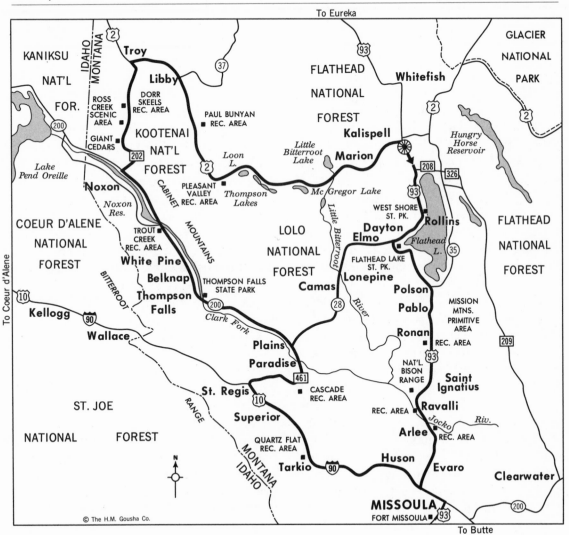

© The H.M. Gousha Co.

Tough Rides in North Wyoming and Yellowstone

On this map are routes to suit every taste and skill. Most cyclists will do well to stay within Yellowstone National Park and explore the many natural wonders. More adventurous souls can take a beautiful ride out the east end of the park and through Shoshone Canyon to Cody, one of the best of the Wild West towns. And cyclists with unusual stamina and unusual bicycles can take a spectacular but awesomely difficult 350-mile loop up into Gallatin National Forest of southern Montana.

Yellowstone is a great place to cycle, if you can cope with crowded highways. The loop shown here starts at West Yellowstone, but actually you can put the bikes on the cars, drive to any spot in the park and start touring. You might be wise to consult with park rangers before starting, to make sure there are no impairments to cyclists. Think twice before taking the ride from Canyon to Tower; the climb is a tough one.

There are 16 improved campgrounds in the park, plus plenty of other accommodations. West Yellowstone is a busy little city, and even has a laundromat where you can also take a shower.

On the way to Cody, you'll find Pahaska Campground just outside the east entrance to the park and Horse Creek Campground, an excellent place to camp near the river. Cody, itself, has many motels and restaurants. The Buffalo Bill Historical Center is housed in log buildings resembling Bill's ranch home. The museum displays many historic mementoes of the Old West.

On the 350-mile loop, you'll see some spectacular country if you can keep the perspiration out of your eyes. This is a grueling ride. There are no campgrounds between Cody and Red Lodge, but several at the latter town. Carry water, because it is scarce. Belfry has a clean little restaurant, and Red Lodge is a major supply center. It's all uphill from Belfry to Red Lodge, except for the last mile; Red Lodge to Park-

Approximate mileage: 100 — Park loop; 200 — round trip to Cody; 350 — Montana.

Best times for touring: Summers only.

Terrain: Very mountainous.

Traffic: Heavy on all Yellowstone roads during peak summer season.

Historical points of interest: Many in Yellowstone; Buffalo Bill Museum in Cody.

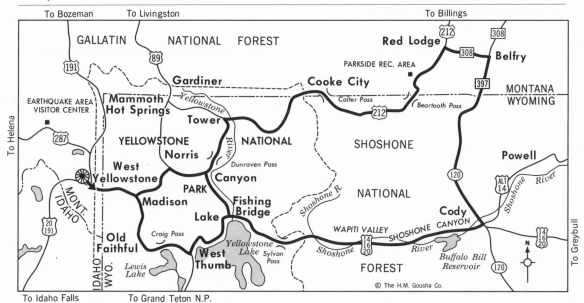

side Recreational Area is all uphill again. The road is excellent, but the hills are always there. The final climb up to Colter Pass is particularly tiring.

Soda Butte campground near Cooke City is inviting; the ride from the camp into Cooke City is all downhill. You can take it easier getting to Tower Junction, but then the 16 miles into Canyon Junction is uphill all the way except the last two miles.

Up in the high country, you'll pass the Twin Lakes and Gardner City Headwalls, still decked in snow and ice in mid-summer. For those who can make it, the feeling when you hit that 10,970-foot summit goes a long way toward relieving the aches and pains of the climb.

Mountains and Mining on Three Boulder Trips

Here are three loop rides out of Boulder, varying in length and difficulty. They're good anytime after the weather warms in spring right through fall's color show.

Boulder is one of the many historic towns in Colorado; it was settled in 1858 and grew gradually as a mining and agricultural center. The state's first schoolhouse was erected here in 1860. The University of Colorado was founded here in 1861.

Rides into the surrounding countryside give you more glimpses of the area's history. The 21-mile loop to Louisville takes you into the coal mining district. The town has four fine Italian restaurants which guarantee a continuous flow of visitors. The Blue Parrot at Pine and Main Streets is friendly with cyclists and has good homemade spaghetti.

The ride to Longmont also stays on the flatlands, but cyclists have excellent views of the 14,000-peaks of the Rocky Mountains off to the west. Longmont has its share of good eating places, too, so you can stop and refuel before pedaling back into Boulder. This is agricultural country, and roads tend to be lightly traveled.

The mountain ride is a route of another character. The elevation at the intersection of U.S. 36 and Lefthand Canyon Drive is 5,600 feet. At Ward, it's 9,300 feet. That's a 3,700 foot climb, and a tough one. But for those who make it, there's the wonderful 3,000 foot drop down to Lyons.

U.S. 36 has a wide shoulder for safe riding between Boulder and Nelson Road. North of Nelson Road, the shoulder narrows and the traffic can be very heavy on weekends. Exercise caution, and try this ride on weekdays if at all possible.

Ward enjoyed some fine boom days as a mining center; one of its mines is supposed to have produced two million ounces of silver during three years.

Approx. mileage: 21, round trip to Louisville; 45, round trip to Longmont; 70, mountain loop.

Best times for touring: Summer and fall.

Terrain: Mostly flat, except mountain ride which has very steep grades.

Traffic: Heavy in Boulder.

Historical points of interest: Longmont, which dates back to 1870; former mining towns in the mountains; Boulder itself.

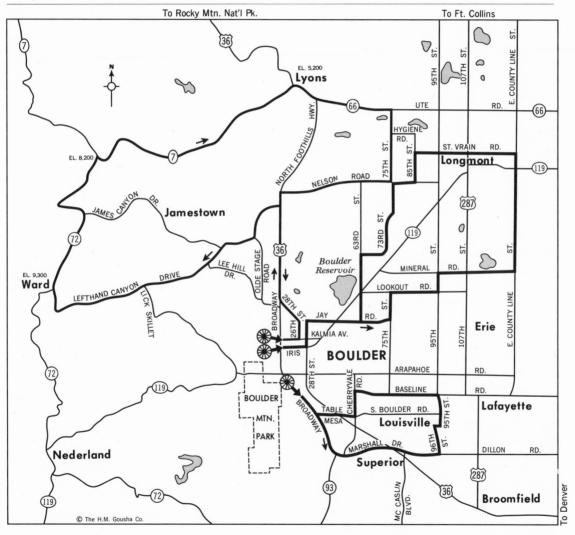

Ketchum–the Heart of Hemingway Country

Pages of *For Whom the Bells Toll* were written in Ketchum, the starting site for this 65-mile ride. Ernest Hemingway made his last home in this small Idaho community and is buried in the town's cemetery.

From Ketchum, follow U.S. 93, one of the few north-south highways in Idaho. A mile away is Sun Valley, known to skiers throughout the world. Originally developed by the Union Pacific Railroad, this area has grown into an all-year recreation site. Nestled in the Sawtooth Mountains, the "American Alps," it previews the beauty of this ride.

From Sun Valley, the route winds up past the 6,000-foot altitude mark. If you are riding in the spring, you will witness a dazzling display of wildflowers. Look for the state flower, the *syringa*, with its white flowers, yellow stamen and tall, bush-like appearance. Summer colors are provided by the columbine dressed in scarlet, yellow,

blue or white. And, of course, autumn has a golden, mellow beauty all its own to please any rider.

As you ride into the Boulder Mountains, notice the abundance of timber. One third of Idaho is forest land. Douglas fir, ponderosa pine, Englemann spruce and western red cedar predominate.

Galena Summit is the height of your ride. Stop to view the majestic scenery as well as to catch your breath in the thin air of this 8,701 foot crest. Much of the land before you is in the same condition as when the Shoshoni Indians lived here. These early settlers called this region "Ea-da-how," meaning "sunup" or "sun descending from the mountains."

Ride past Alturas Lake and toward Redfish Lake and Recreation Area as you continue to pedal north. The Redfish Lake Visitors Center presents historical, geological and naturalist displays and dioramas. Free guided

Approximate mileage: 65.

Best times for touring: All year, except winter.

Terrain: Mountainous.

Traffic: Moderate.

Historical points of interest: Ketchum, where Hemingway lived and is buried.

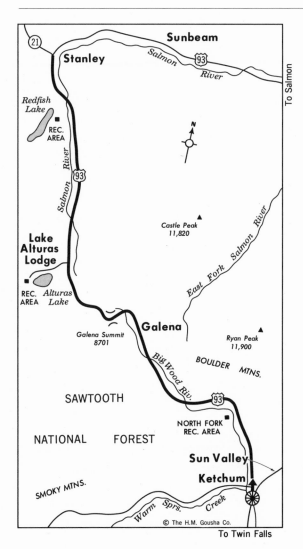

To Twin Falls

tours are given daily from June 15 to September 15.

You may also catch glimpses of the animal life around this area. Where herds of prehistoric mammoth, mastodon and musk ox roamed, deer, elk, antelope, caribou and a multitude of smaller game now live.

From Redfish Lake, it is only another five miles to the trail's end at Stanley and the Stanley Basin Recreation Area. The town is a left-over settlement from the picturesque Old West, born during the gold strikes of the 1880's.

The Salmon River, called the "River of No Return" by the Indians originates in this basin. Fed by mountain streams and snow, this waterway contains trout, salmon, perch, sturgeon and bass.

Plan to park your bike here, and picnic among the beauty of Idaho before starting on your return trip to Ketchum and Sun Valley.

A Ghost Town and Cherry Trees in Idaho

Boise is the starting point for a ghost town ride, and another tour through Idaho's cherry country and recreational areas.

Boise is the state capital and largest city. Before taking off enjoy a guided tour through the Capitol Building. Other points of interest in the city include: Julia Davis Park (zoo, rose garden, picnicking, boat rentals), Ann Morrison Memorial Park, and St. Michael's Cathedral.

The first tour takes State 21 to Idaho City. About 10 miles along the route is the Lucky Peak-Sandy Point area, where you can take a dip, have a picnic and even camp overnight. Further up the route is Robie Creek, which also sports swimming and picnic grounds. In this stretch you will have a thousand foot climb. All along the route, which begins paralleling Mores Creek about the 15 mile point, are beautiful spots for stopping and enjoying the scenery.

The end of your pilgrimage is the ghost town of Idaho City. Once a booming gold rush city, the town now caters to tourists. An added hot attraction is the warm springs open all year long. Unless you have arranged transportation back to Boise, plan to camp along the route.

For tour two it is best to leave Boise in the early morning to get over the major climb at Horseshoe Bend as early as possible. State 52 parallels the Payette River, offering lovely scenery and picnic areas.

This is fruit country, with rolling hills bearing huge annual crops. Let your taste buds bloom if it's spring and you are heading for Emmett, famous for its cherries.

Because popular recreational areas are destinations on this ride, it would be wise to avoid weekends and holidays, if possible.

Approx. mileage: 70, one way—Boise to Idaho City; 80—Emmett Valley loop.

Best times for touring: April-November; best at cherry time.

Terrain: Mostly easy cycling with a few steep hills.

Traffic: Heavy in recreation spots on weekends.

Historical points of interest: Boise, Idaho City ghost town.

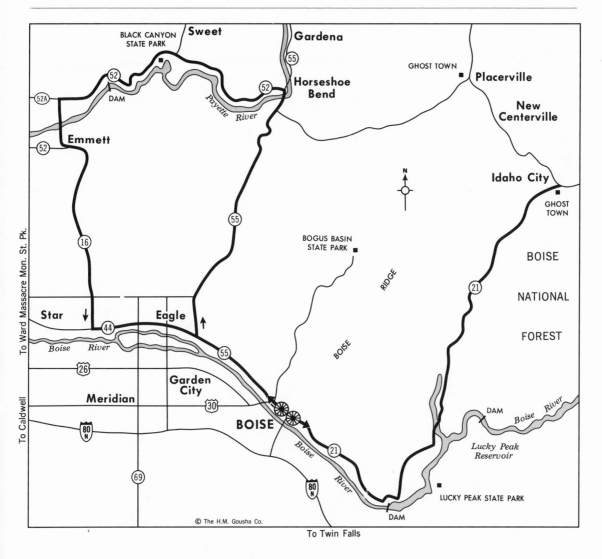

A Utah Alpine for the Experts

Before you tackle the 37-mile alpine loop in the American Fork Canyon, you should have enjoyed several shorter tours with less strenuous mountains. This is a high altitude trip for experienced cyclists. No services are available between the departure point and U.S. 189.

The tour begins at Timpanogos Cave National Monument off State Route 80. A steep trail leads one and one-half miles up the side of the mountain to the cave, climbing to 6,730 feet. The cave's limestone formations are fascinating and chilly. Take a jacket.

From here the route takes State 80 through the wild beauty of American Fork Canyon. Mount Timpanogos overlooks the cyclist as he loops and switches for a little over 12 miles to the 8,000-foot summit at Aspen Grove. This family recreation area is a good spot to relax and have a snack.

The south end of the alpine loop switches back and forth sharply past the Sundance recreation area. A mammoth ski resort is operated here under the watchful eye of movie star Robert Redford who along with a few associates owns the area. From here the route picks up U.S. 189 and drops into broad Provo Canyon. Bridal Veil Falls is a spot worth stopping for. The famous aerial tramway lifts you from the canyon floor to what appears a mere speck of a restaurant perched at the edge of a sheer cliff overlooking the misty falls floating down to the waiting river in two graceful cascades.

Follow the Provo River through the canyon which offers the cyclist a variety of diversions: fishing, camping, tubing on the river.

The tour takes State Route 52 out of the canyon to U.S. 89 past Pleasant Grove to State Route 146. There are numerous camping opportunities. Follow State 146 past Helsetts Hollow up to State 80. Head east here back to Timpanogos Cave National Monument.

Approximate mileage: 37 mile loop.

Best times for touring: June, July, August, September-before cold fall weather.

Terrain: High elevation, steep grades over paved route. Recommended for the experienced cyclist.

Traffic: Sometimes heavy on weekends and holidays.

Historical points of interest: Timpanogos Cave National Monument, Bridal Veil Falls.

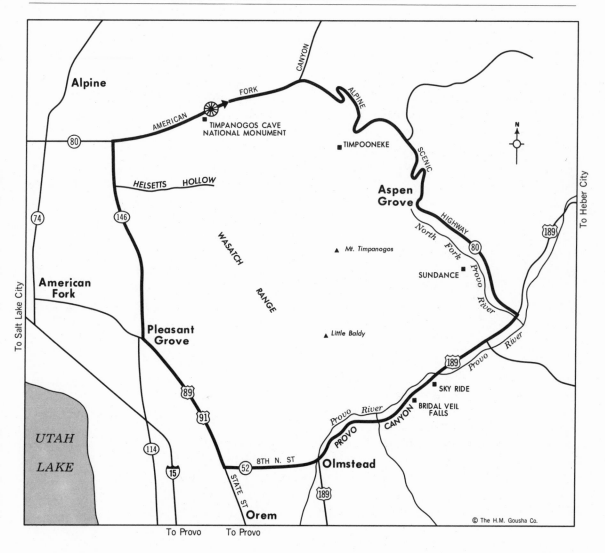

© The H.M. Gousha Co.

Long Weekend Excursion Into Cache Forest

This double century, plus 29 miles loop through the Cache Forest is perfect for a three day weekend excursion. The high altitudes and some steep grades can tire even the experienced cyclist, so pace yourself.

The tour begins in Ogden, the second largest city in Utah. About four miles south on U.S. 89 is the John M. Browning Armory and Firearms Museum, a fabulous collection of old guns.

Take U.S. 89 and 30S through farming country to Brigham City. Named for Brigham Young, the Mormon colonizer, the city houses an antique collection in the County Courthouse.

(A 30-mile optional ride to Bear River Migratory Bird Refuge heads west.)

The route follows U.S. 89-91 out of the city, climbs Sardine Canyon and later crosses the southern end of the Cache Valley before it continues to Logan. The twin gray towers of the Mormon Temple and tree-shaded Utah State University dominate this city. After the long trek a nice snooze will be welcome.

After a good breakfast in Logan, head northeast on U.S. 89 through Logan Canyon. You will pass varied tree types and rugged rock walls jagging into the sky. At the 7,805-foot summit is a panorama that includes Bear Lake.

Forty miles north is Garden City and Bear Lake State Park, a good place for camping, fishing and a refreshing dip.

State 30 swings down along the south lakeshore to Pickleville and Laketown before reaching Sage Creek junction. The tour now takes State 16 through high country to Woodruff. Motels are available here. Take State Route 39 westward back into the Cache Forest. This is a scenic route that rolls along the willow-bordered stream of Walton Canyon where beaver frolic by their underwater dams. The road continues on to the Monte Cristo campgrounds.

This is important ski country, so keep in mind the possibility of a return in winter.

Approximate mileage: 229; optional loop trip, 30.

Best times for touring: Mid-June to mid-September.

Terrain: Paved road, steep climbs over Sardine Canyon to the summit of Logan Canyon.

Traffic: Heavy on weekends on major roads.

Historical points of interest: Bear River Migratory Bird Refuge, John M. Browning Armory and Firearms Museum, Brigham City, Utah State University, Mormon Temple.

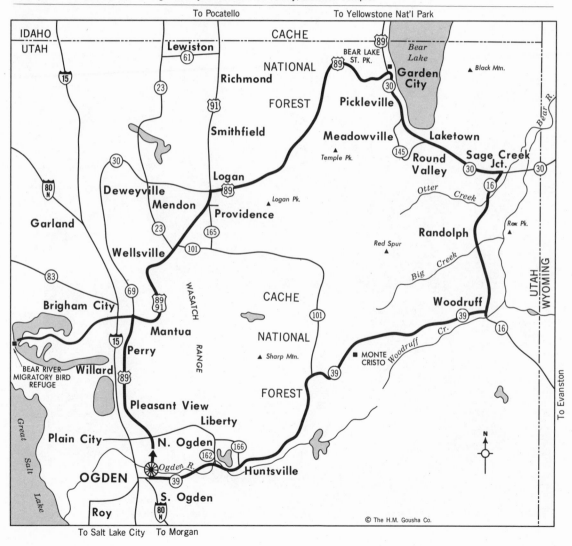

Southwest

Hit the Will Rogers Trail in Oklahoma

Will Rogers, cowboy humorist and rope twirler par excellence lives again on this Oklahoma to Kansas tour.

The tour begins in Oklahoma City off Int. 35. Motels are available all over town and there is a campground at Chisholm Trail Park, eight miles east of the Capitol Building, on U.S. 81.

In Oklahoma City, first visit the capitol building and grounds. Of particular interest is the oil well directly under the building.

For those who always dreamed of riding off into the sunset the Cowboy Hall of Fame should corral your attention. Western artifacts and pioneer gear, a history of all the major old west trails, a display of a championship rodeo stars' equipment combine with a large museum.

Then head out toward Sapulpa. There is a campground 12 miles southwest on U.S. 66 at Heyburn Reservoir.

Tulsa, built on the banks of the Arkansas River is one of the more beautiful western cities. Oral Roberts University, built on the verbal energies of the famous preacher, is situated near the entrance to the city.

Next stop on the cowboy cruise is Claremore. This is considered the hometown of Will Rogers since it is the nearest town of any size to the place he was raised. Visit the Will Rogers Memorial. Enclosed by a beautiful park, a stone building houses much of Rogers' personal items and informative displays on his life.

A multi-million dollar gun collection, one of the largest and finest in the world is on display at the Gun Museum in the city.

Pedal lazily through the rolling countryside to Oologah. Near here is Will Rogers' boyhood home and the ranch where he grew up. Camping at Oologah Reservoir and Will Rogers State Parks.

Time to mount up and head on out. Last stop is Coffeyville, Kansas, where the Dalton gang bit the dust.

Approximate mileage: 200.

Best times for touring: April through October; midsummer is terribly hot.

Terrain: Good paved roads with many short hills.

Traffic: Heavy traffic for about five miles in both Oklahoma City and Tulsa.

Historical points of interest: Capitol Building, Cowboy Hall of Fame, Will Rogers hometown, Will Rogers' Memorial, Gun Museum, Coffeyville.

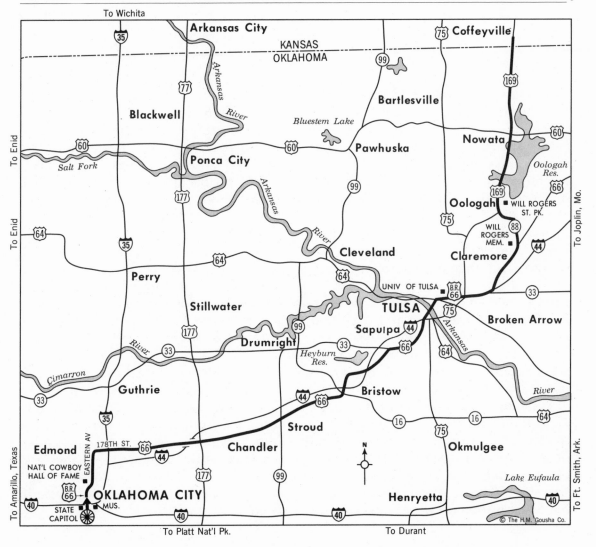

A Trio of Tours in the Bluebonnet Country

Here are three possible routes for delightful rides through the colorful bluebonnet country of Texas about midway between Austin and Houston. For maximum enjoyment, time your ride when the flowers hit their peak. If you want to check at the last minute, phone the Washington County Chamber of Commerce in Brenham.

The Chappell Hill tour route has good roads with minimum traffic. Many of the original buildings in town have been preserved, including the Lockhart Plantation built in 1850 and the Stage Coach Inn dating from 1847. The Masonic Cemetery is worth visiting, to see headstones of some of the area's more famous citizens.

Washington-On-The-Brazos State Park is the end point of this loop. It is the site of the Anson Jones home built in 1845. Dr. Jones was the last president of the Republic of Texas. Here, too, is the old Hatfield Plantation. A new historical museum can occupy you for a couple of hours or more with its films and artifacts.

There are two possible loops out of Brenham. The shorter heads north to Gay Hill and the circles to Independence and back. The longer starts out to the southwest, then makes a long loop through Burton and on to Independence for a total of about 75 miles.

The town of Brenham was founded in 1843. It has developed as a farming and trade center, and serves as the main supply spot for cyclists, with motels and restaurants. St. Peter's Espiscopal Church was originally dedicated in 1848 and rebuilt in 1965.

Independence has the site of Old Baylor College, established in 1845.

As you tour this country, you'll notice a European atmosphere not only in the towns but also in the countryside. Virtually all the towns and villages got their start as German or Polish settlements, and the mother tongues are still spoken.

Approx. mileage: 40 on the Chapel Hill tour; 30 on the short Brenham tour; 75 on the long Brenham tour.

Best times for touring: April, when the bluebonnets are blooming.

Terrain: Mostly flat, with some rolling hills.

Traffic: Satisfactory, except for Highway 50 near Brenham.

Historical points of interest: Chappell Hill and Brenham, historical markers along all routes.

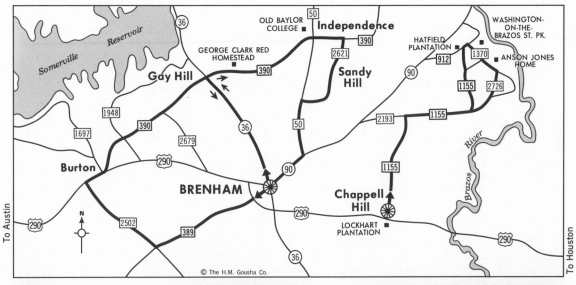

Big Texas Loop Ride Through the Hill Country

Things come big in Texas and this 225-mile loop tour through the Hill Country is no exception. Rolling hills, frontier museums, L. B. J. country and glass bottom boats combine to make this one enormous cycling adventure.

The tour begins in New Braunfels, accessible via Interstate 35. This Germanic town was founded in 1845 by Prince Carl von Solms-Braunfels, Commissioner-General for the Society for the Protection of German Immigrants in Texas. The Prince, obviously more concerned with his own affairs than with protecting immigrants, abandoned the town because he couldn't live in courtly style there.

Relics of pioneer days are at the Sophienburg Memorial Museum. It is open daily during the summer and on Mondays and Fridays the remainder of the year. For a little relaxation before heading out, stop at Landa Park.

Mount your bike and ride out of town on State 46 through Boerne. A few miles south of the town is the Cascade Caverns with interesting fossil and rock formations. (At Boerne you can take alternate rides indicated on the map.)

The next stop is Bandera, off State 16. Formerly a Mormon settlement the town now possesses a real Western frontier atmosphere. At the Frontier Times Museum early Texas and frontier items are on display.

The route takes Road 173 to Road 480 into Center Point, then picks up State 27 and Road 783 into Comfort and Harper. You might want to spend the night here. From Harper ride along Road 2093 into Fredericksburg, the birthplace of Fleet Admiral Chester W. Nimitz. Fredericksburg is the home of the Nimitz Memorial Naval Museum.

The Pioneer Museum and Country Store contains relics of the German colonists who fought Indians, disease and the Civil War to settle in the area. Many motels are available with the

Approximate mileage: 225.

Best times for touring: Spring or fall.

Terrain: Rolling hills.

Traffic: No problem.

Historical points of interest: Frontier Times Museum, Blanco Museum, Pioneer Village, L.B.J. country.

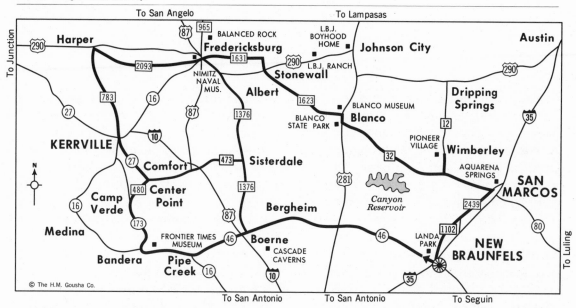

Sunday House being the best and the most expensive. Restaurants abound, serving up Texas style portions of American and German dishes.

Here is a chance to take an L.B.J. Ranch loop trip on U.S. 290 and U.S. 281. You will also pass Johnson City, boyhood home of the late President Lyndon Johnson.

The regular tour continues along Road 1623 through Blanco. Here, there is a museum and the Blanco State Park.

Next day ride State 32 from Blanco to Wimberley and Pioneer Village. Such frontier delights as a Gay 90's show, Tonic and Medicine Show and a reproduction of an 1880 town await any dude with enough coin.

The last stop before heading home is San Marcos and Aquarena Springs. Glassbottom boats glide over clear springs at this watery peeping-tom land.

From here follow the route back to your original stomping ground.

Spanish Flashback in Sunny Albuquerque

Riding through Albuquerque is a trip into 250 years of history. The Spanish, Mexican, Confederate and, finally, American flags have flown over this city. In 1706, Don Francisco Cuervo y Valdes, the area's governor, resettled thirty families here because of the good pasture land for their sheep.

With the majestic Sandia Mountains and the warm sun your constant companions, begin the ride from the University of New Mexico's 500-acre campus. Visit the exhibits and museum here, for they will acquaint you with the background of this region. Some of them are the Maxwell Museum of Anthropology, the Museum of Geology, the University Art Gallery and Popejoy Hall, center for Albuquerque's performing arts. All are free.

From the University travel west on Lomas Blvd., passing the Civic auditorium and crossing the Atchison & Topeka and Santa Fe railroad tracks. The completion of these rail systems in 1881 did much to spur the small town's growth.

Continue to Central Avenue and famous "Route 66," leading east to Chicago and west to Los Angeles. Here, however, it will take you to Old Town Bridge to cross the Rio Grande River. This great waterway flows through the center of New Mexico, providing much-needed irrigation for the dry land.

The city's second university, the University of Albuquerque, is along Coors Blvd. as you pedal northward. Be sure to see La Luz and the Indian Polytechnical Institute before turning on to Corrales Rd. Both are excellent examples of how modern dwellings can complement the natural landscape.

On the return loop, plan to stop and spend a few hours in historic Old Town. This is where the city originally began. However, when an Old Town landowner refused to sell his land to the railroad, an alternate track route was laid, leading to the birth of New Albu-

Approximate mileage: 25.

Best times for touring: All year.

Terrain: Generally smooth with a few hills.

Traffic: N. Coor has poor shoulders and fast traffic; other streets are fairly wide with lighter traffic on Sundays and holidays.

Historical points of interest: Old Town, University of New Mexico.

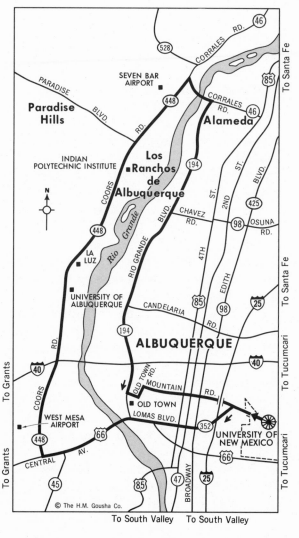

querque to the east. That town's growth soon surrounded the original settlement.

With its grass-covered plaza, gas lights and wrought-iron bandstand, Old Town is a blend of Indian, Spanish colonial and Western Victorian styles. One of the landmarks of the Plaza is San Felipe de Neri, also established in 1706. This church has never missed a single Sunday Mass.

Browse through the many shops selling traditional Indian and Spanish arts and crafts as well as contemporary wares. And try sampling some of the food.

The Old Town Fiesta is held during the first weekend in June while New Mexico's Arts and Crafts Fair is held here on the first weekend in August. You may want to plan your ride to include either of these colorful events.

New Mexico 173

Coronado Slept Here and Searched for Gold

Coronado searched for the "seven golden cities" on his exploration of New Mexico in 1540. You may not find gold along this 40 mile loop but the trip will pan out as a cycling experience you won't forget.

This is an easy ride; plan to spend the entire day on the tour, packing a lunch, riding out to the Coronado State Monument. Have a picnic, see the grounds and leisurely pedal home. Be sure you take along sun glasses as New Mexico sun is glaring.

Begin the tour in either Old Town or the University of New Mexico in Albuquerque.

The old Town Plaza has a lovely Spanish flavor, with many shops and restaurants. University of New Mexico is an exceptionally beautiful campus with a good museum.

Follow the map out to the Coronado State Monument. Coronado and his men rode into this vast, 1,200 room pueblo in 1540. They found a large system of rooms, called *kivas* (underground prayer rooms), and hundreds of Indians. Today many of the rooms remain very clearly marked and well-maintained. There is an excellent museum here along with the painted kiva in which excavators have found some of the finest frescos in the United States.

Coronado and his men were seeking the fabled seven golden cities of Cibola on his journey to this area; unfortunately he failed in his search but you may have better luck if sightseeing has made you hungry or tired. There are a couple of good hamburger stands nearby and immediately adjacent to the ruins are many campsites on the shore of the Rio Grande. When Will Rogers saw the Rio Grande, he said, "It's the first river I've seen that needs irrigating."

The route loops around back toward Albuquerque through Bernalillo. In this town was the beginnings of Albuquer-

Approximate mileage: 40.

Best times for touring: Any season. During winter check weather conditions.

Terrain: Easy ride.

Traffic: Moderate; heavy in Albuquerque.

Historical points of interest: Coronado State Park and Monument.

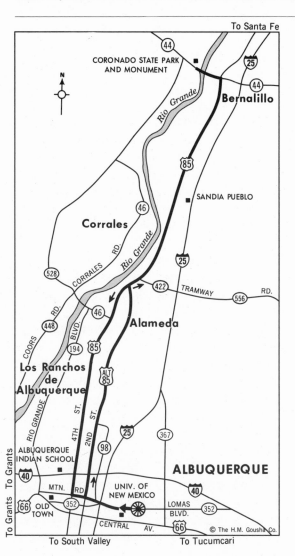

que. In 1706 Don Francisco Cuervo y Valdes, then the governor of New Mexico, moved thirty families from Bernalillo to a homestead 15 miles south on the Rio Grande where there was better pasture land. He named the community after the Duke of Albuquerque.

Follow the map and the tour will loop back to the departure point.

Explore Grand Canyon's Breathtaking South Rim

"**No matter how far** you have wandered . . . the Grand Canyon will seem novel to you . . . as if you had found it on some other star", John Muir wrote after his first visit in the 1890's. Spaniards from Coronado's party in 1540 had discovered the canyon and reported its inaccessibility.

Explored by John Wesley Powell first in 1869, the Canyon was visited by Pres. Theodore Roosevelt, who was instrumental in naming it a National Park in 1919.

Tourists on bicycles really aren't common among the one and a half million who visit the Canyon annually. Most cyclists bring their bikes in on car racks and enjoy a personal perusal of the spectacles from the South Rim.

A 35 mile, one way ride, this tour edges the gorge from the Desert View entrance station to Grand Canyon Village and on west a bit to Hermits Rest. The road is fairly level, with the expected curves and small slopes. Be forewarned: the Park rangers point out that all the roads are narrow, but paved and wide enough to accommodate bikes. They are *very* heavily traveled. Stay on the shoulders when possible. For obvious reasons, most of them vertical, there is no bike riding below the rim.

Although the South Rim road is open all year, there usually is snow in the winter. Rangers advise September and October for bike touring. During those months the weather is best, the fall color dominant and the hordes have thinned a bit. Spring also is a good time. In July and August there will be thunderstorms, perhaps too exciting if you are on a bike hanging out over a 7000 foot deep canyon.

Accommodations are plentiful, ranging from the luxurious old El Tovar to more moderately priced motels. No reservations are needed for the campgrounds. One is near the Visitor Center at Mather and the other adjacent to the bike tour's starting point at Desert

Approximate mileage: 37.

Best times for touring: Spring and fall.

Terrain: Mostly flat along the Rim with a few gentle slopes.

Traffic: Roads are very heavily traveled; 1½ million visitors yearly.

Historical points of interest: Grand Canyon, (20 million years old), Visitor Center and Museum, Tusayan Ruin.

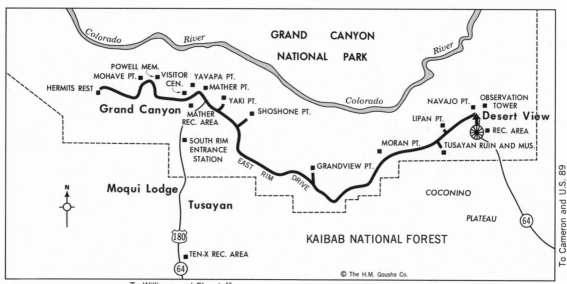

View. You can camp among the junipers and pines and buy supplies at the store in the village.

If you arrive at Grand Canyon via State 64 from the east you will have your first view at Desert View. Unload your bikes and start from here. (This East Rim Drive section is open only in summer.) Take a tour of the prehistoric ruins at Tusayan Ruin and Museum, built about 1200 A.D.

From a bike you will have fantastic views of the gorge. Moran Point was named for Thomas Moran whose painting of the point hangs in the Capitol in Washington. Grandview, Yaki, Mather and Yavapai are overviews before you get to Grand Canyon Village.

The Visitor Center here is devoted to the history and geology of the area and has a museum with dioramas.

At the end of the tour, Hermit's Rest affords magnificent views across the Canyon.

Past Dude Ranches to Old Vulture Mine

The Vulture Mine is one of the most intriguing spots in Arizona. It was discovered by German mineralogist Henry Wickenburg in 1863, and its prosperity accounted for the birth and rise of the town of Wickenburg. By 1866, the town was one of the largest settlements in the entire Arizona Territory, and missed being named territorial capital by only two votes.

The mine itself is private property. When it's open, you can see the site of the gold-rich diggings and the machinery that's still in place. The road out to the mine site winds between picturesque mountain and desert scenery.

Actually, you have a choice of two tours here. You can start at Sun City and pedal the 34 miles along U.S. Route 60 to Wickenburg before striking out on Vulture Mine Rd. If you feel less adventuresome, drive right to Wickenburg, park there, and shorten your trip to a bumpy 19 miles in each direction. In either case, be ready for the last 10 miles of the road to the mine site. It's good gravel but not recommended for tubular tires. And be especially careful after a rain; this area is prone to flash floods.

A good starting point at Sun City is the Suntower Coffee Shop at 108th Ave. and Grand Ave. From there, you need only go left on Grand Ave. to catch Route 60.

Sun City is historical in its own right; it was the first of the really successful senior citizen communities in the U.S. and even today it stands out as the shining example of this kind of development.

Don't be surprised if you find yourself straining a bit on the way to Wickenburg. You climb about 1,000 feet in the 34 miles, from an altitude of about 1,100 feet at Sun City to 2,100 feet at Wickenburg. You'll be even higher at the mine, but the absence of any steep hills makes the climb relatively painless, unless it is very hot.

Approx. mileage: 105, complete round trip; about 28, round trip between Wickenburg and mine.

Best time for touring: Spring, fall, and winter; summers not recommended because of heat.

Terrain: No major hills, but a gradual increase in altitude; rough gravel road to the mine.

Traffic: Quite substantial on U.S. 60.

Historical points of interest: The Vulture Mine; Wickenburg, traditionally the center of Arizona's dude ranch country.

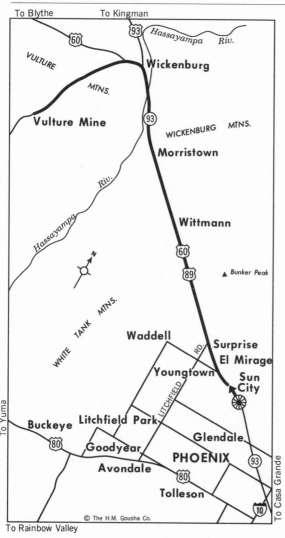

Route 60 fortunately is wide enough to accommodate bicycles without much danger. Weekdays are always best for a trip like this, but with care, you can negotiate the route on all but the busiest Sundays.

Even though the best spots are picked over, the Wickenburg hills are famous for their bottle hunting possibilities. Should you stop for a rest along the way, poke around a bit and keep an eye open—the rare specimens bring high prices with collectors.

The Old West in Historic Phoenix

Outlined here is a giant circle tour of the Phoenix-Scottsdale area, with short loops at either end for those who want to cover the territory in shorter circles.

A good part of the route follows side streets to keep bicyclists away from the heavy traffic of arterials.

An ideal place to start in downtown Phoenix is the State Capitol at 17th Ave. and Washington St. This handsome old structure was built around the turn of the century of stone native to the area.

The Arizona Museum has more mementoes of the earlier days, and includes a good bit on Indian history.

Encanto Park makes an excellent rest or picnic spot, with its lagoons, shaded lawns and playgrounds.

In the shopping center on the north side of Indian School Road between Central Avenue and Third Avenue, seek out the Bayless Cracker Barrel Store Museum. It preserves some of the best of the "good old days."

Heard Museum has some spectacular collections of Indian artifacts, including an unsurpassed display of Kachinas.

Lincoln Drive is the route chosen for the long loop to Scottsdale, both because of its good condition and for the views it affords to cyclists and motorists alike. If you've never seen Camelback Inn, it's worth a few minutes of your time to ride in and look around.

Scottsdale delights most visitors with its Old Western charm, and you may be tempted to stray off the official path to look around at all those wagon wheels and stone buildings.

At the southeastern end of the tour, you can return to Phoenix via Oak St., making a long swing through colorful Arizona State University.

If you want to ignore Phoenix altogether, you can start the tour in Papago Park, ride up to Scottsdale for an hour or two, visit Arizona State and then return to the park.

Best times for touring: Spring and fall are best; avoid the summer heat; check on wind before trying a long winter ride.

Approx. mileage: 40 for the big loop; about 11 each for the downtown Phoenix and Scottsdale trips.

Terrain: Generally flat, with some mild hills between Phoenix and Scottsdale.

Traffic: Slight on the side streets, heavy on the arterials, downtown areas.

Historical points of interest: Arizona Museum, Heard Museum, State Capitol, Bayless Museum, Pagago Park.

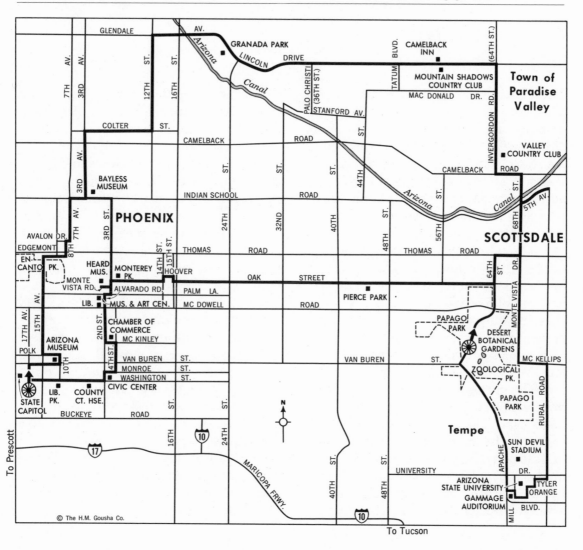

© The H.M. Gousha Co.

Loop Past the Scenic Adobes in Old Tucson

These two tours in the city of Tucson take you to the city's most historical sections, and to some of the best bits of history in the entire Southwest. They are short enough for an easy day's ride, and the strong-of-will might want to put them together for a very long day of non-stop touring. Both start at Pueblo Center for convenience sake, but you can pick up either loop anywhere.

The Mission loop has San Xavier del Bac as its keynote, and deservedly so. You're not likely to find such a remarkable building in such an ideal setting anywhere else in Arizona (or along California's Mission Trail, for that matter). But there are other good spots, too. The entire area around the Church St. and Washington St. intersection is filled with old adobes from the 19th century. The best block for viewing the buildings is bounded by Main, Alameda, Meyer and Washington Streets. Just to the west, in the Paseo Redondo area, you'll find another important residential section, this one dating to the early 20th century when this was "the" place to live in Tucson.

You can ignore Sentinel Peak altogether if you aren't anxious to do any climbing. But the view from the top is spectacular, and many cyclists find it worth the extra effort.

Near the intersection of Grande St. and Mission Lane are the sites of the town's first grist mill and the first church, St. Augustine Mission.

On the return leg of this loop, pay particular attention to the old residential areas on either side of Tenth Ave.

The ride to Fort Lowell takes you out through residential Tucson on a leisurely ride to the famous ruins of the old fort, which was built in the 1870's as a key defense post in the continuing wars against the Apaches.

The return leg passes through the University of Arizona, where you can stop and view artifacts of prehistoric life in the Arizona State Museum.

Approximate mileage: 16 on the downtown Fort Lowell loop, 18 on the Mission San Xavier loop.

Best times for touring: Spring and fall are best, but winter is fine unless windy and rainy.

Terrain: Flat, except the sidetrip to the top of Sentinel Park.

Traffic: Fairly light in the residential areas, but downtown area and around the University can be choked with cars.

Historical points of interest: Adobes dating back to the 1800's, Mission San Xavier del Bac, the excellent Arizona State Museum on the University campus, ruins of Fort Lowell.

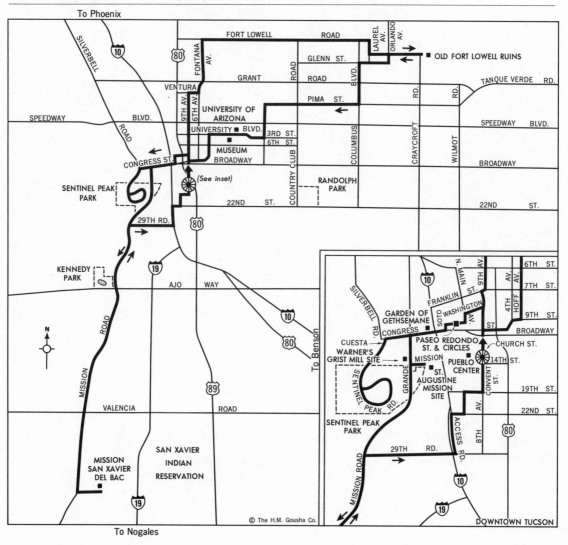

© The H.M. Gousha Co.

Far West

Ghost Town Bonanza In Wild West Nevada

Some ghost towns have spirits of another variety, too, and on this 25-mile tour to Virginia City you may quaff heartily at an authentic boomtown saloon while contemplating the ghosts of the rip-roaring past.

The tour begins at Carson City, the capital of Nevada. The city was first called Eagle Ranch and was later named after the famed scout Kit Carson. During the gold and silver rush days the city became the social center for the nearby mining towns and gained notoriety as a Wild West action-packed community. Some of that flavor still hangs on—important interests are gambling and horses.

A former U.S. Mint, the Nevada State Museum in Carson City exhibits coins, guns, minerals, mining tools and Indian artifacts. A 300-foot mine tunnel runs beneath the building. Open daily 8:30 to 4:30; free.

"The Life of the Fireman," an exhibit at Warren Engine Company Museum, contains old photographs, antique fire-fighting equipment and the state's first fire truck. Open daily; free.

The State Capitol Building constructed in 1871, at N. Carson St., is a large stone structure with hewn logs of great length for its rafters.

After sightseeing, take U.S. 50 out of Carson City, eight miles to State Route 17 and head north to Gold Hill and Virginia City. Go about three miles and take a left onto State Route 80 to Silver City and Gold Hill.

Gold Hill, along with Virginia City, is one of the best and largest authentic examples of a western mining metropolis. Practically all the buildings and many of the residences date back to the boom days. The combined population of the old sites totalled close to 70,000 and over a billion dollars worth of silver and gold, has been excavated here since the mid-1800's.

Buildings like the Bank of California, opened at Gold Hill in May, 1865, still

Approximate mileage: 37.

Best times for touring: Avoid summer and early fall. It's hot!

Terrain: Flat around Carson City; several miles of serious hills near Virginia City.

Traffic: Some congestion in Carson and Virginia City. Look out for fast cars on U.S. 50.

Historical points of interest: Carson City, Nevada State Museum, Gold Hill, Virginia City.

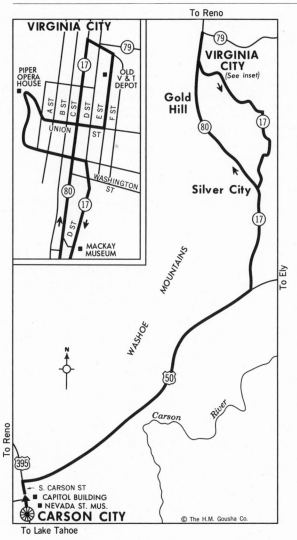

stand as a reminder.

"Queen of the Comstock," Virginia City is the most celebrated and liveliest ghost town in the world. Once one of the richest cities in North America, its dazzling career coincided with the life of the Comstock Lode, one of the richest mineral finds in history. In the 1870's during its heyday, Virginia City had four banks, six churches, an opera house, numerous theaters, 110 saloons and the only elevator between Chicago and San Francisco. Mark Twain was a news reporter here and some great fortunes, including that of William Randolph Hearst, were founded at the mines.

This "ghost town" today does a booming tourist trade and offers many unusual attractions from the wild gold rush days. Piper's Opera House, the baroque mansions of the silver kings and ten ornate saloons date back to the 1870's.

The tour returns to Carson City via State Route 17 and U.S. 50.

Nevada 187

Las Vegas Glitter and Two Desert Rides

In 1844, Capt. John C. Fremont wrote of "a camping ground called Las Vegas." Located along the Old Spanish Trail, it was also the site of a Mormon lead mine. The land was later purchased for $18 from the Paiute Indians. From such mild and modest beginnings, Las Vegas has developed into a neon-lit stage of gambling casinos and celebrities and is the start for the following two tours.

Tour no. 1 begins at Main and Lake Mead Blvd. Bring a water bottle with you since it is 45 miles to more water. Heading east into the colorful desert, you will encounter the only difficult climb of the ride at Frenchmen Pass. Then pedal to Lake Mead North Shore Road, turn left and follow the edge of this 3,000-square mile lake. The cliffs and ridges ranging from grey to red and purple provide color.

Midway on this tour is the Valley of Fire, known for its bright red sandstone. The years have shaped the rock walls into eerie camels, elephants and faces. Stop at the Interpretive Center at the main entrance for information on the Indian petroglyphs.

From U.S. Route 40, ride southwest to Int. 15. You must ride on the freeway here, so stay on the paved shoulders until the Ely turnoff and the frontage road.

Before reaching Las Vegas, you will pass the southernmost tip of the Atomic Energy Commission's Nevada Test Site.

Tour no. 2 begins on Industrial Blvd. behind the famous Las Vegas "Strip." Turn onto Blue Diamond Road, which you will ride most of the way, as it circles around in the Red Rock Canyon Recreation Lands. At Willow Springs see the site of Indian camps dating back to 700 A.D.

The general store in Blue Diamond is a good place to stop and view the wind swept sandstone bluffs comprising the southern extension of the Spring Mountains.

Approximate mileage: Tour no. 1: 100; Tour no. 2: 45.

Best times for touring: Early spring, late fall. Short days in winter, but nice weather. Hot summers.

Terrain: Hilly.

Traffic: No speed limit on highways, so watch for traffic.

Historical points of interest: Tour no. 1: Las Vegas, Valley of Fire, Nevada Test Site; Tour no. 2: Red Rock Canyon, Willow Springs.

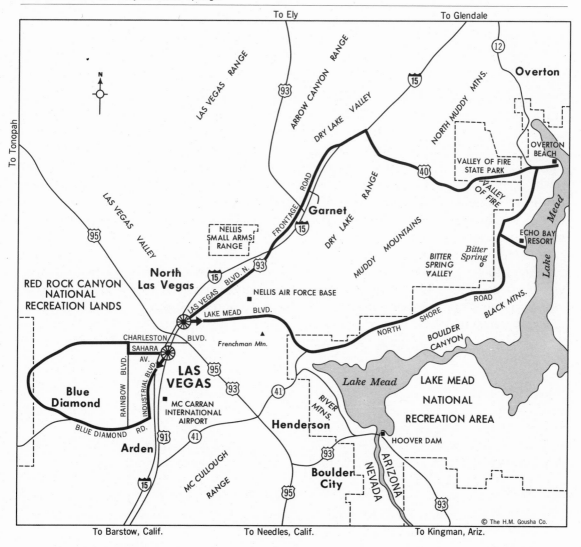

© The H.M. Gousha Co.

Mexican California History in San Diego

This San Diego tour combines history and a salty breeze for a pleasant 30-mile ride.

Pepper Grove Drive in Balboa Park is a good starting point. Ride west on El Prado till you come to First Ave., then north to Washington. Turn left and follow the signs to Presidio Park, a fine vantage point.

Going down the hill, you will pass Fort Stockton on the left and the Serra Museum on the right. The famous Mormon Battalion billeted here in 1847. The fort has one of the two guns used in the defense of the town in 1846. The Serra Museum gives a fine view over Mission Valley and Point Loma.

Halfway down the slope towards Old Town, you will see excavations. This is the site of the Spanish presidio which functioned here from 1769 to the 1820's. When you get to the bottom of the hill, turn left on Taylor, go a few blocks, and turn left on San Diego Ave., which is the access road to Old Town Plaza, an historic spot where Lt. Rowan raised the American flag on July 29, 1846, without Mexican opposition.

Spend a few minutes on the Plaza. The Estudillo house dating back to the 1820's is worth a visit, as are other historical sites.

From here retrace your path to Taylor then take Rosecrans St. out to Sports Arena Blvd. and go right to Midway. Follow the route, (passing Sea World and heavy traffic), around Mission Bay and tour the outskirts of the water area according to the map.

The route below Mission Bay takes South Mission Bay Drive to Sunset Cliffs Blvd. The tour continues out to Sunset Cliffs.

A steep climb up Hill St. paves the way to the Loma peninsula. Pedal out to the Cabrillo National Monument.

The homeward route retraces back to Catalina St., then to Canon St. Make the Shelter Island and Harbor Island loops, then take North Harbor Drive.

Approximate mileage: 30.

Best times for touring: Any season.

Terrain: Mostly flat.

Traffic: City traffic is always a hazard but not especially serious except at key intersections.

Historical points of interest: Fort Stockton, Serra Museum, Old Town, Estudillo house, Presidio Park.

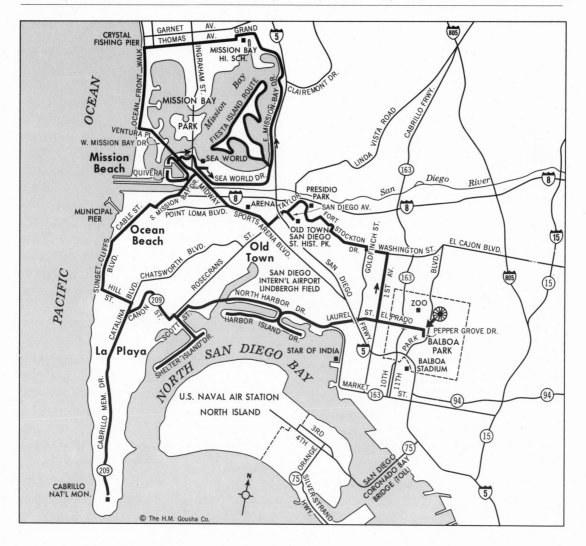

Pastry Tour Past Mission Santa Ynez

A word of warning opens this tour—don't settle down at a table in one of Solvang's excellent Danish restaurants before you start. You might decide suddenly to scrap the tour and just eat your way around town.

Head out of town to Ballard Canyon Rd. Ballard Canyon is an opening to the rolling ranch country. The route becomes Foxen Canyon Rd. after you cross State 154 and the ranchland views along here are superb. From Foxen swing left onto Alisos Canyon Rd. for a little exercise over some moderate grades.

Show some care when you reach U.S. 101. The traffic is speedy, but the well-paved shoulder makes excellent riding. Six flat miles later you head east on State 154 for a spectacular view of the wildflowers, if you are touring in the spring.

In the old town of Los Olivos, Mattei's Tavern gives you a chance to quench your thirst and think about the early day carryings-on around here. Los Olivos grew up as one of fifty California stops on the famed Butterfield Stage Line from Missouri to Los Angeles and north to San Francisco.

The stages (top speed 15 miles per hour under good conditions) enjoyed brief, colorful fame just before the Civil War. The line ended abruptly at the war's end with the opening of the railroad which spanned the continent. Mattei's Tavern was built in 1886 on the site of the local Butterfield stop.

Back on your bike you will ride along the Old San Marcos Pass Rd. (State 154) for a few miles, turning right on the road into Santa Ynez. Past the town turn in to the lovely Mission Santa Ynez, built in 1804. Now beautifully restored after decades of misuse and ruin, this mission is one of the most beautiful in the chain that Father Serra developed in California. The museum contains well-preserved early Spanish and Mexican California relics, and a

Approximate mileage: 40.

Best times for touring: Best in spring when wildflowers bloom, but good all year.

Terrain: Moderate hill climbs and flat canyon roads.

Traffic: Light, except U.S. 101 and Solvang.

Historical points of interest: Mission Santa Ynez, Mattei's Tavern, Solvang.

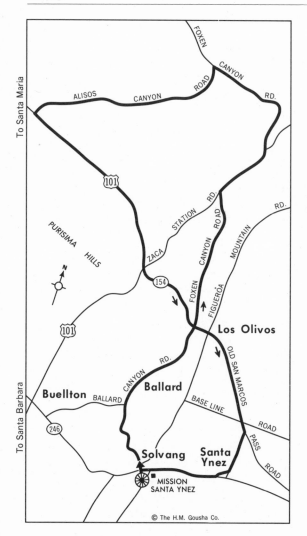

horse fiddle and a mechanical organ.

Now swing back to Solvang. After you have a taste of pastry or a meal and browse around the shops filled with Scandinavian handcrafts, you may decide to spend another day in this unique town established in 1911 by a Danish teacher and a preacher as a community for, of course, Danes. The Scandinavian architecture, customs, crafts, food and festivals of Solvang have made it a pleasant and unusual tourist attraction.

There are many pleasant motels in this area and off U.S. 101 south. Another Southern California tour that is nearby will take you along the Pacific Coast into the historic city of Santa Barbara. See page 194.

Along the Pacific to Sunny Santa Barbara

Perpetuating mission architecture and early California history, Santa Barbara is the destination of this oceanside tour. From the beach community of Carpinteria to Santa Barbara, which spreads from a gently curving beach back to the rugged Santa Ynez Mountains, the round trip is an easy 30 miles along slightly traveled roads that run parallel to U.S. 101.

In Carpinteria, starting at Linden, follow Carpinteria Ave. to soon cross over U.S. 101. Via Real North is the route you will follow, passing the Santa Barbara Polo Club and a curious Santa Claus a few miles up the way.

Entering Santa Barbara from the east is a pleasure. Montecito, with its elegant homes set in a landscape thick with trees, is a cyclist's delight. Follow this route: right off Coast Village Rd. onto Hermosilla Drive; then left off Hot Springs Rd. to Old Coast Highway. Soon you pass the country club on your right, tennis courts on the left and after a short ride enter the main section of Santa Barbara.

Take Salinas St. to Carpinteria St. where you turn left. Then ride right on Milpas, left on Gutierrez and right again on State St., the heart of the city.

Downtown Santa Barbara is a museum in itself with preserved adobes, Presidio Real, El Paseo pedestrian arcade. True to early tradition, the Spanish architecture is echoed in the arched and towered court house and museum of art.

A complete walking (or cycling) tour of Pueblo Viejo (Old Town) and information on other historical sights, is available from the Chamber of Commerce at 1301 Santa Barbara St. You may have time to take a ride out to the lovely Mission Santa Barbara, the "queen of the missions."

Lunch on Mexican food at one of the many good places downtown. There are outdoor cafes in the vicinity of El Paseo, where you can also window shop.

Approximate mileage: 30.

Best times for touring: Excellent any time of year.

Terrain: Mostly flat on rural roads that parallel the Pacific.

Traffic: Heavy in Santa Barbara.

Historical points of interest: Presidio Real, El Paseo Pueblo Viejo, Santa Barbara Mission.

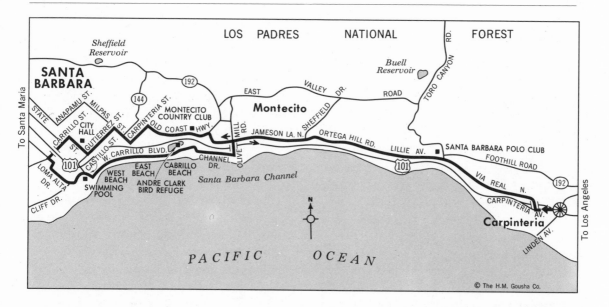

Just a few blocks from the route at 115 De La Guerra is Hazard's Bike Shop, a stronghold for cyclists since 1914. It is one of the best stocked shops in the West and capable of making any repairs.

Follow Carrillo St., crossing under the freeway, to Loma Alta Drive, Cliff Drive and Castillo St., out to West Cabrillo Blvd. and the palm-lined waterfront. Along here you will pass postcard views—with grassy parks, sailboats, artists and swimmers. Past restaurants, gift shops and periodic art exhibits in the East Cabrillo Blvd. section of the waterfront, follow the well marked bike path along the Andre Clark Bird Refuge.

The fabled Santa Barbara Biltmore is on the ride after the bird refuge. Pick up Olive Mill Rd. and cross over the U.S. 101 freeway to retrace your route back to Carpinteria.

Ride the One Way Roads of Yosemite Valley

Yosemite's discovery by whites came in 1849 when a pair of miners were tracking a bear they had wounded. By 1855 the first tourists had followed the Indian trails for a look at the grandeur, and John Muir and other conservationists became alarmed about the commercial development. Interest was aroused in Congress and in 1864 President Lincoln ceded the area to California "for public use, unalienable for all time."

Bicycling in Yosemite Valley is much more enjoyable now than it was a few years ago. The entire east end of the Valley is closed to auto traffic, so cyclists can pedal along in peace except for an occasional shuttle bus. And in the western part of the Valley, the roads are one way.

The two tours shown on the map are short and if you do nothing but ride around the loops, they can be finished in short order. But that's not the way to enjoy Yosemite Valley. Instead, pack a picnic lunch and start out from Yosemite Village. Plan on spending a day on the road, stopping to throw a few rocks into the Merced River, enjoy the views, or take one of the short hikes to the waterfalls.

On the eastern loop, the natural stopping point is Mirror Lake. But you can also spend some time profitably at Happy Isles, one of the Valley's major trail heads and the location of a comprehensive information center.

On the return leg, be sure to stop at Indian Cave, where you can clamber around on the rocks and take the easy three-mile trail along Tenaya Creek. This isn't a very tiring walk, and it affords some spectacular new views of Half Dome.

The longer loop has a worthwhile stop every half mile. There are many excellent guidebooks available for your use; perhaps the most practical is the official *Yosemite Road Guide*, which has keyed explanations to every important

Approximate mileage: 5, round trip to Mirror Lake; 12, round trip to Pohono Bridge.

Best times for touring: Good any time the Valley floor is free of snow.

Terrain: Flat with a few mild slopes.

Traffic: East end closed to autos; all one-way roads.

Historical points of interest: Yosemite Valley, created by the Ice Age. Information at Visitors Center.

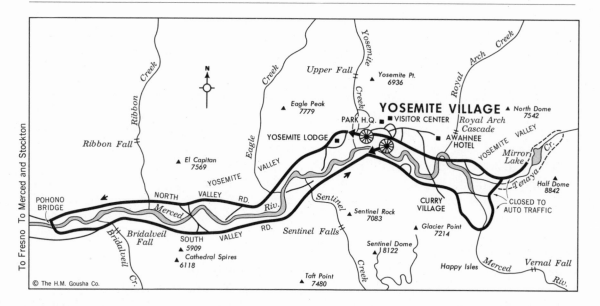

landmark, viewpoint, waterfall and historical site.

There are three excellent spots for lunch on this tour. At El Capitan, Yellow Pine and Rocky Point picnic areas, you can ride down to the edge of the Merced River and get away from most of the sights and sounds of traffic.

If you're making your first trip to Yosemite, spend some time at the main Visitor Center. Here is the story of Yosemite, product of the Ice Age, and

you can get a good introduction to the geology and the flora and fauna of the Valley. Rangers on duty will tell you about the best view points and the trails suited to your individual hiking.

Accommodations range from the elegant Ahwahnee Hotel down to rustic cabins. Several campgrounds also are available. There is a full range of services at Yosemite Village and Curry Village, so you can easily replenish your food and clothing supplies.

Monterey Peninsula Scenic Bayside Tour

The village atmosphere of Carmel, the forests and mansions along the famed Seventeen Mile Drive, the rock-bound coast of Pacific Grove and the early Mexican California buildings in Monterey highlight this tour.

The name most often associated with the California Franciscan Missions is that of Father Junipero Serra. He founded San Carlos de Borromeo, known now more simply as Carmel Mission, in 1770. From this beautiful location at the head of the Carmel Valley, Father Serra directed the business of the Missions. Upon his death in 1784, he was buried in the sanctuary.

Enjoy the museum and gardens and start your ride to Carmel, crossing State 1 and staying with the roads closest to the beach. Along the Carmel Bay stretch, the village's spectacular homes and the older gingerbread cottages are nestled.

At the top of the steep Ocean Ave. business district is a park on the corner of Junipero Ave. This makes an excellent stop for lunch, especially because of the gourmet Mediterranean Market across the street.

Retrace the steep Ocean Ave. hill and pick up the route via San Antonio Ave. and Carmel Way to the Seventeen Mile Drive toll gate. As this renowned road is closed to cyclists on weekends and during special events like the Crosby Golf Tournament, call ahead to Del Monte Properties, (408) 624-6411.

Past Pebble Beach Golf Course and the beautiful Del Monte Lodge, ride around Point Pescadero that juts out into Carmel Bay and gives a fabulous look back at the shimmering waters.

The Lone Cypress, trademark of the whole area, is a good resting point. Just north of Cypress Point Golf Course is one of the most beautiful beaches on the entire ride, Fan Shell Beach, and Bird and Seal Rocks.

Out of Seventeen Mile Drive you are in the town of Pacific Grove. Take the

Approximate mileage: 35.

Best times for touring: Good throughout the year on weekdays. Seventeen-Mile Drive open to cyclists during the week *only*.

Terrain: Gently rolling; several hills.

Traffic: Congested in Carmel, Monterey.

Historical points of interest: Carmel Mission, Cannery Row, Custom House in Monterey.

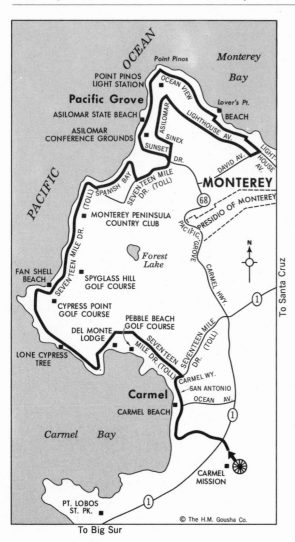

To Big Sur

inland route through the tree-lined residential area to Lighthouse Ave., where you pass the Butterfly Trees. Here the Monarchs spend every winter. Or opt for more coastal scenery and ride through Asilomar State Park past the ocean sculptured rocks and tide pools.

Rounding Lovers Point you'll see in the park a statue of a butterfly commemorating Pacific Grove's famous winter residents. Along Ocean View are Victorian homes, giving an entirely different atmosphere from Carmel. Stay on the streets close to the water and you will come to Cannery Row, made famous by John Steinbeck.

From David Ave. you may choose to continue on into Monterey to visit the wharf, the Custom House and the many adobe dwellings, relics of a Spanish and Mexican era.

Bicentennial Birthday Ride In San Francisco

San Francisco's 200-year old Spanish beginnings will be celebrated in 1976. The Presidio and Mission Dolores, stars of the bicentennial, are the historical points on this tour of more than a quarter of San Francisco.

The Mission Dolores sidetrip can be made right at the start. You will run into a few steep spots as you near the Mission, founded June 29, 1776, five days before the revolutionaries on the other side of the continent issued the Declaration of Independence. The squat little church is filled with relics and sits in garden overlooked by a statue of Father Serra.

Ride past the glass Conservatory on the regular route through part of Golden Gate Park. Take the Sixth Ave. exit and turn back to Fifth Ave. There is a steep hill just before the Presidio, 1500-acre military reserve established two centuries ago by Juan Bautista de Anza. You can walk your bike through a small gate into the Presidio and con-tinue along Arguello Blvd. past shady lanes and the old adobe officers' club.

Fort Point is the outstanding feature. On a rocky headland it juts out into San Francisco Bay, massed under the immense approach to the Golden Gate Bridge. The old Spanish fort was razed in 1854 and the current brick mass was patterned after Fort Sumter, South Carolina.

Lincoln Blvd. and El Camino del Mar take you past luxurious homes up a wide steep hill to the Palace of the Legion of Honor, combining a location of breathtaking beauty with a fine collection of European art.

Pass Seal Rocks and the Cliff House and follow the route around Lake Merced and back into Golden Gate Park. Transformed from "a dreary waste of sand hills" the huge park includes a museum complex and Japanese Tea Garden and miles of bike paths to be explored.

Approximate mileage: 25 miles; Mission Dolores trip, 6 miles.

Best times for touring: All year, except in fog.

Terrain: City streets, good-sized hills, bikepaths.

Traffic: Jammed on weekends and commute hours.

Historical points of interest: Presidio, Mission Dolores, Golden Gate Park, Palace of the Legion of Honor, Seal Rocks.

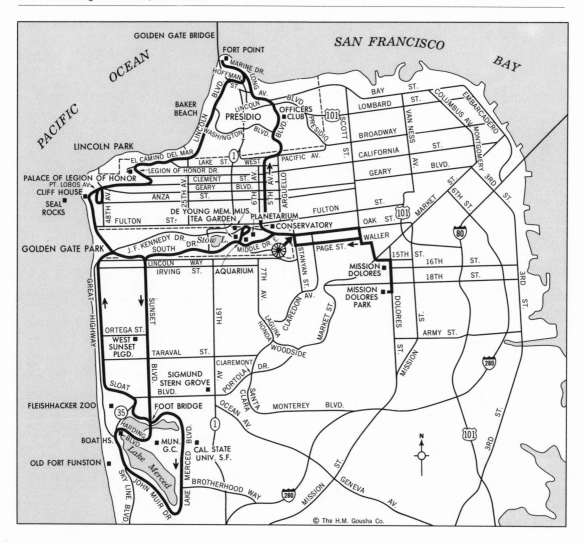

Ride the Pacific's Craggy Oregon Coast

Sea breezes, craggy cliffs and the crashing surf blend with a rich heritage to make this 145-mile tour down Oregon's famed coast unforgettable cycling.

The two-day tour begins in Astoria. Called by its residents the "Oldest American City West of the Missouri" the city is steeped in history. One first it can claim is the first post office west of the "Big Muddy." In judging age, Astoria can rightfully declare itself old, as white men came as early as 1792.

The tour takes U.S. 101 out of Astoria. Thirteen miles to the west, out on the jutting peninsula, is Fort Stevens. Built in 1846, the battery emplacements still stand with 19th century houses and barns as neighbors.

A few miles out of Astoria to the south is Fort Clatsop National Monument, the restored stockade of the Lewis and Clark party. A visitors' center contains a graphic historical presentation of the entire Lewis and Clark expedition.

Later on the route be sure to visit the end of the Lewis and Clark trail at the Salt Cairn. U.S. 101 continues to Seaside, Oregon's most popular beach.

Cannon Beach, eight miles south, is best known for Haystack Rock, one of the largest monoliths in the northwest. Five miles further U.S. 101 rounds a spectacular cliff on the face of Neah-Kah-Nie Mountain.

The nearby town of Rockaway is a good place to spend the night. The Silver Sands Motel is recommended.

In the morning the tour continues to Tillamook. This rich dairy area, laced with diked rivers has been dubbed "Little Holland." The Cheese Factory and The Pioneer Museum, with an outstanding collection of wildlife photos, are must stops.

Out of Tillamook is an alternate 19-mile loop which offers some of the most spectacular scenery on the coast.

At Hebo the route takes State 22 over the coastal range to Salem.

Approximate mileage: 145.

Best times for touring: Anytime except the rainy season.

Terrain: Twisty runs along the coast, some hills inland.

Traffic: Can be a tight squeeze on U.S. 101.

Historical points of interest: Astoria, Fort Stevens, Fort Clatsop National Monument, Tillamook.

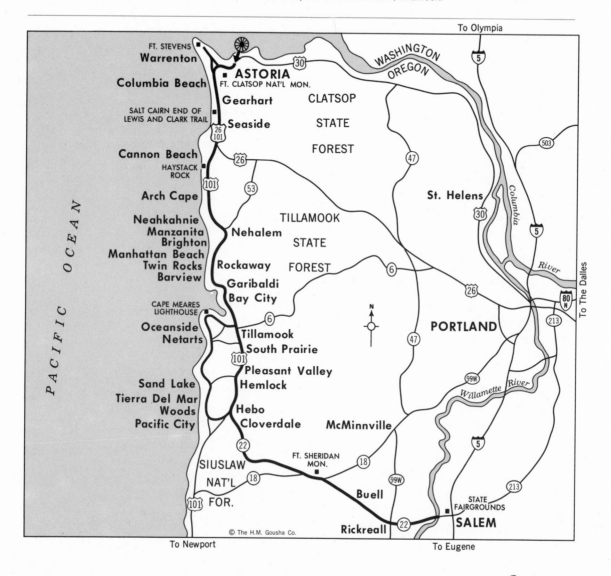

© The H.M. Gousha Co.

Ride the Back Roads from Salem to Champoeg

This 50 mile tour takes the cyclist from the capital of the Beaver State through back roads to one of its most important historical landmarks, Champoeg Park.

Begin at the Fairgrounds in Salem, heading east on Silverton Road. At the stop light at Lancaster Dr. go left and head north to Portland Road. Take a right here onto the bikeway and continue north to Hazelgreen Road. Go right and after about 5 miles, head north on Howell Prairie Road. (Or, ride the route to Mt. Angel, which could be an interesting sidetrip. A monastery was established on the Mount by the Order of St. Benedict in 1883. Saint Mary's Parish Church, a modified Gothic structure stands in the middle of Mount Angel. The view is a spectacular panorama of the valley below.)

Back on Howell Prairie Road, the route crosses U.S. 99E. A short ride further and you come to Gervais. This Oregon town was established when the Oregon & California Railroad, now the Southern Pacific, was built through the valley in 1868–72. The town was named for Joseph Gervais, in whose home was held the "Wolf Meeting" that led to the formation of an American local government.

Crossing Int. 5, continue to Woodburn when the route takes Road 65 north through Broadacres to Donald.

Continuing on Road 65 (which becomes Butteville Road), turn left on 414 and follow the signs to Champoeg State Park.

Here, when the whites arrived, was an Indian village at a place called Cham-poo-ick because of an edible plant of the same name growing there in abundance. The village was headquarters of the local chieftain and the point where the scattered tribesmen gathered before setting off on hunting expeditions. For this reason, William Wallace and J. C. Halsey came down from Astoria in 1811 and established a crude trading post for the Pacific Fur

Approximate mileage: 50.

Best times for touring: Any time except the rainy season.

Terrain: Country roads and some hilly areas.

Traffic: Take care on State Routes 99E and 219 and in Salem.

Historical points of interest: Champoeg State Park, Mount Angel church.

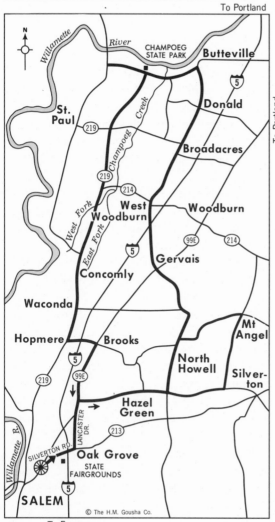

Company. Gradually the number of buildings increased and the area became one of the chief settlements in the valley.

Today at Champoeg State Park are two museums that trace the history of the area. Also there are nice grounds for a picnic lunch.

Leave the Park, ride up the hill, across the intersection and head south on Road 8, which will become State 219. Take a left turn toward Brooks. At Brooks turn right on State Route 99E and pick up the bikeway as you enter the Salem area on Portland Road and retrace the route to the fairgrounds.

Plunging Waterfalls, A Great Dam and Mount Hood

Water falls, legends, a great dam and the looming presence of Mt. Hood are offered on this 160 mile loop through Oregon.

The tour begins at the Portland airport. Take State 213 to N.E. Sandy Blvd. which will become U.S. 30.

Past Lewis and Clark State Park take the scenic route past Dabney State Park to Crown Point. Here, in the comfort of the Vista House perched 725 feet above the Columbia River Gorge, you are treated to a magnificent view.

Continuing along the scenic route, it may seem that raindrops keep falling on your head but it will really be the cool mist from the waterfalls that dot the area. Latourell Falls is just a short distance from Crown Point and is the first in a series of watery cascades. Bridal Veil Falls, Wahkeena Falls (picnicking here) and the most famous, Multnomah Falls, fill the air with the crashing sound of a plunging river.

(Inexperienced riders are encouraged to turn around at Multnomah Falls and head back to Portland to avoid the strong easterly winds in the Columbia River Gorge.)

The route continues on Interstate 80 past the Bonneville Dam. If the salmon are spawning, watching the slippery struggle up the fish ladders is exciting.

Near the dam is the Bridge of Gods and the Cascade Locks. This area is steeped in history and legend. Visit the Cascade Locks Museum. On display is the first steam locomotive used in the Oregon territory and information on all facets of transportation.

Passing through the Columbia Gorge the route takes U.S. 30 to the Hood River. State Route 35 heads south from here passing Panorama Point and a host of state parks before it heads west becoming U.S. 26. This area is rich in scenic camping spots where you may rest for the night with enormous Mount Hood commanding the landscape. Pick up a campsite map at any of the Oregon State Parks for specific information.

Approximate mileage: 160.

Best times for touring: Spring and summer.

Terrain: Good secondary roads, hilly.

Traffic: No problem. Expect strong easterly winds in the Columbia River Gorge.

Historical points of interest: Cascade Locks, Bonneville Dam.

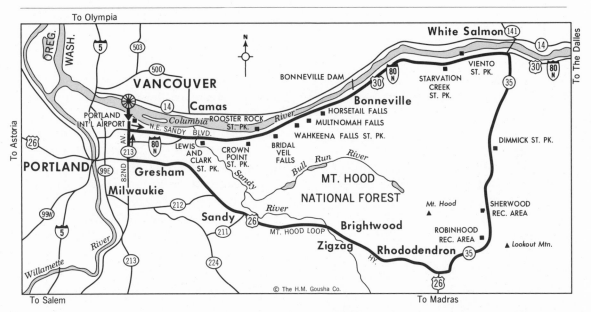

Petrified Trees, Indian Relics on a Two-Day Trip

This two-day loop tour through Washington is one of varied contrasts; the cyclist will pass through an atomic works reservation, visit an Indian museum and a petrified forest.

In warm weather bring plenty of water and salt pills to avoid dehydration as there are some stretches without water stops.

From Vantage take State Route 243 south along the Columbia River. Vantage bridge is posted "auto only," but it is the only way to cross the Columbia.

The ride continues through the sagebrush desert past Beverly and Desert Aire to the Priest Rapids Dam, which you may also tour. From here head east to the junction of State Route 24 and then turn south. The route passes through the Hanford Works U.S. Atomic Energy Commission Reservation, then starts west.

Along this route, just past the junction with State 241, is a cafe where you can eat lunch before continuing on to Yakima.

Continue through Moxee Valley to Yakima. There are motels and cafes on First St. for weary travelers.

The county of Yakima ranks first in the U.S. in the production of apples. Since the early days of irrigation begun in 1875, orchards and farms have replaced sagebrush desert.

The Yakima Museum has a mineral collection, vehicles, Indian artifacts, period costumes and weapons.

You will have to ride Int. 82 for two miles, but there are good shoulders. Out of Yakima take E. Selah to U.S. 97 along the Yakima River to Thrall. Go east on Thrall Rd. to Clemans Rd. and then right to Kittitas where you'll pick up an unnumbered road to Vantage.

Follow this road and the signs to Ginkgo Petrified Forest State Park. Paths through the forest area lace through fossils over 15 million years old. From here it's a quick trip on the route to the departure point at Vantage.

Approximate mileage: 150.

Best times for touring: Spring or fall. Temperatures can reach 120° in summer.

Terrain: Some long hills. Route follows Columbia and Yakima Rivers. High winds not unusual along the Columbia River.

Traffic: Interstate 82 must be traveled for two miles, otherwise traffic not a big problem.

Historical points of interest: Yakima Museum, Ginkgo Petrified Forest.

Three-Day Circle Around Mount Rainier

The Indians called it "The Mountain That Was God," and Mt. Rainier probably had a similar impact on the first white man to see it, Captain George Vancouver. For later Washington pioneers it became a legendary landmark.

Experienced Northwest cyclists describe this loop as "the best tour of the year." The 170 miles take at least three days over good mountain roads.

Weather is chancy at Mount Rainier, but you can expect early July to the second week in October to have clear, warm days.

Day 1: Start this incomparable tour at Enumclaw. There is a big parking lot at the King County Fairgrounds. Ride south a short distance and turn right on Mud Mountain Road. After riding a few miles on State 162, you pass a fish hatchery and shortly afterwards see a sign for Electron.

Continue to Kapowsin where there is a grocery store and tavern. Follow the route to Eatonville where you'll find

Babe's Cafe a good place to stop for lunch. Take the Alder cutoff road to State 7 and 706. Passing Ashford, you come to Copper Creek Lodge. Stop for dinner. It is just a short hop further to a motel or AYH hostel.

Day 2: Stop frequently today to enjoy the spectacle; later see the Visitor Center displays at Paradise. Ohanapecosh campground is the place to spend your second night.

Day 3: Head to Cayuse Pass and the White River Entrance to the Park. Shortly, there is a chance to take a side trip to Sunrise (a 3,000-foot climb.) The downhill runs are fabulous. Make a lunch stop at Silver Springs.

Stay on State 410 past The Dalles campground. Soon you'll see a wood timbered overpass with an oil-surfaced Weyerhaeuser logging road running to the left. Take it to avoid the heavy traffic on 410. Be sure to leave this road at the last exit before it goes under Mud Mt. Road. Otherwise you will end up at the sawmill.

Approx. mileage: 170 (Day 1-67, Day 2-44, Day 3-59).

Best times for touring: July–October. First week in October is preferable.

Terrain: Approximately 9,000-foot elevation gain.

Traffic: Heavy during summer, less after Labor Day.

Historical points of interest: Glacier exhibits, history of Mt. Rainier in movies, slides at Paradise Visitor Center.

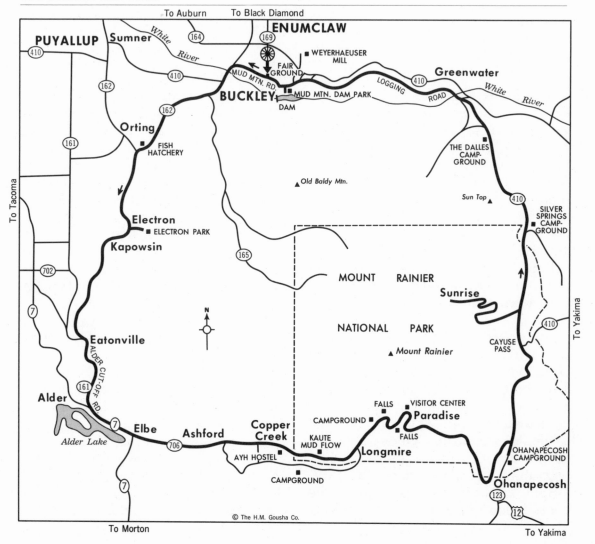

Fighting Salmon and Beer on the Olympia Run

This 38-mile excursion through western Washington is highlighted with a salmon run, a beautiful lake, a state capitol and a brewery.

The tour begins at Millerslyvania Memorial State Park (accessible off Interstate 5, to State 121 and north on Tilley Rd.) The park has 835 acres along Deep Lake, with boating, fishing and swimming facilities.

Ride Tilley Rd. to State 121. The route heads west through Maytown and Little Rock, then goes north on Endicott Road.

Just across U.S. 101 go right on Mix Rd., left on Kaiser Rd., then a quick right on Walnut. Follow Walnut to Division St. and head south to Fourth St. Follow Fourth into Olympia.

Nestled between Mt. Rainier and the Olympic Mountains, Olympia is the capital city of Washington. The first legislature convened here in 1854, despite Indian unrest which forced the construction of a 15-foot stockade surrounding the city.

The buildings which comprise the Capitol Group are located on Capitol Way between 11th and 14th Avenues. Also here is the Capitol Grounds with Japanese cherry trees; an exact replica of Tivoli Gardens fountain in Copenhagen, Denmark; sunken gardens and the First World War Memorial.

At 211 W. 21st Avenue is the State Capitol Museum. Here in a former mansion are displays and exhibits on the state government and history.

The tour retraces the route back to Fourth St. and takes the Deschutes Parkway along Capitol Lake. At the dam on the lake you can see thousands of fighting salmon making their way upstream during the spawning season (starting in mid-August).

At Tumwater Park just off the Parkway is another good view of the salmon; up the street on Custer Way the Olympia Brewing Company conducts tours and passes out beer.

Approximate mileage: 38.

Best time for touring: Any season, except in rainy weather.

Terrain: Easy grades except one short steep hill.

Traffic: Parkway avoids the major traffic at Olympia.

Historical points of interest: Capitol State Museum.

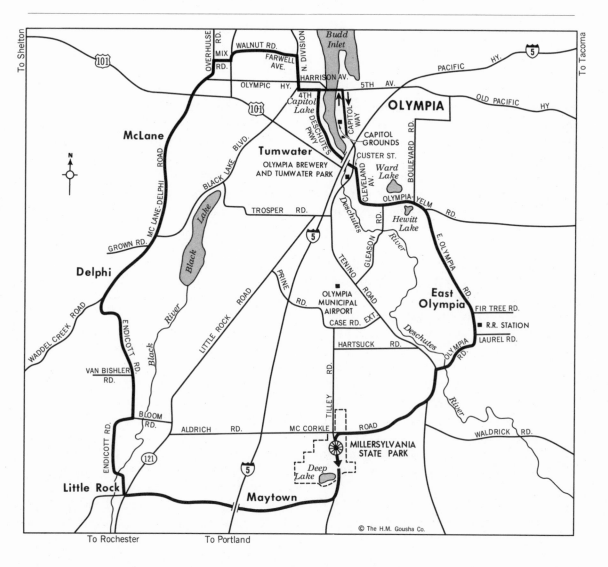

© The H.M. Gousha Co.

Puget Sound Double Century, Via Victoria

Ferry rides, lush forests, islands and a jaunt into British Columbia are all part of this bicycle bonanza through Washington's Puget Sound.

This loop tour goes from Seattle, the Space Needle city, to Canada's port city of Victoria. The area was first explored by Captain George Vancouver when he sailed his ship *The Discovery* into the unchartered region in 1792. He named it Puget Sound in honor of his third-in-command, Peter Puget.

The first day of the trip you will ride 53 miles from Seattle to Port Townsend.

Pedal down to Pier 52, check the schedules and take the 45-minute ferry ride to Bremerton. At Bremerton follow the one-way traffic route for two blocks, then take a right on Pacific Ave. After another five blocks, go left on 6th (State 304), left on Callow for five blocks; right for two, then three blocks to the *U.S.S. Missouri.*

Located next to Pier G, the *U.S.S. Missouri* was the scene of the surrender that terminated World War II. Tours. Admission $1.25.

After visiting the ship return to Calley and 6th. Turn north on State 3 and continue about 20 miles to the floating bridge and State 104. Across the bridge take the side road to Chimacum and Port Townsend.

There are camping facilities at Port Townsend State Park four miles south of town. Points of interest are the Chinese Tree Heaven and the Crown Zellerbach Corporation. At the campsite is an old fort established in 1856, which saw some activity during the Second World War.

The second day of the tour you have the option of taking State 113 and returning to Seattle along U.S. 101 or continuing on to Victoria, B.C. For those adventurers who want to push on, take the ferry to Keystone. Travel along the old road to Oak Harbor (it will join State 525) to Deception Pass Bridge State Park. This area is noted for its

Approximate mileage: 200, about half by ferryboat.

Best times for touring: Any time except the cold rainy season.

Terrain: Varied—highways, forest roads, and steep grades at times.

Traffic: Moderate to heavy in some places.

Historical points of interest: *U.S.S. Missouri*; Port Townsend; Victoria, B.C.

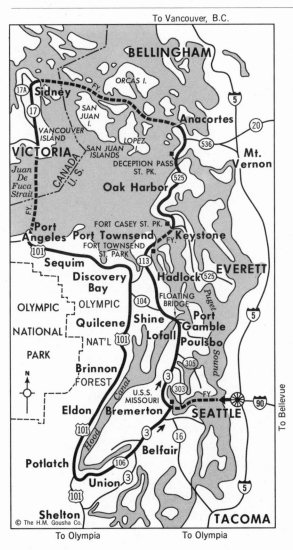

varied land and seascapes; it's also a good place for a refreshing swim.

Outside the park, past the lake, take Deception Rd. up the steep grade to Gilbralter Rd. Go north to Scatterlee Rd. then on to Summit Park Rd. Follow the route to State 536 and into Anacortes. There are restaurants and motels.

The next day take the International Ferry through the San Juan Islands. It's a good idea to catch the 8 a.m. ride as the next one doesn't leave for two and a half hours. At the end of the ride in Sidney you will go through customs. Leaving the city head south on Route 17. From here you may want to take the four mile side trip to Butchart Gardens. There are camping areas all along the route; watch for signs. Route 17 will take you into Victoria, with historic buildings and gardens.

The last day take the ferry to Port Angeles and ride U.S. 101 all the way down the Hood Canal, where you pick up State 106 to State 3 and back to Seattle.

Mountains and Beaches on Kauai's North Shore

The North Shore of Kauai offers this beautiful 45-mile tour past a host of perfect beaches, sugar and pineapple fields and a variety of unusual churches.

Kauai was the first of the Hawaiian islands to be discovered by the famed explorer Captain Cook—and among the last to be rediscovered by modern day travelers.

The tour begins at the Lihue Airport on State 570 and heads north on State 56. A few miles past the airport there is an optional sidetrip to Wailua Falls. Take one of the river launches for a three-mile cruise to the falls. At the end of the boat ride the passengers disembark to explore the caves at the hauntingly beautiful Fern Grotto.

Back on the route continue along State 56 past the Hanamalu Beach Park turnoff. Continue following the coastline in places, to Wailua River State Park. State Route 580 heads west from here and offers a short seven-mile loop trip to Opaekaa Falls and the Sleeping Giant. The name Opaekaa means "rolling shrimp" and dates from the days when swarms of shrimp rolled in the turbulent waters at the base of the falls. State Route 581 loops from the falls back to the main route. On the way you will pass the Sleeping Giant, where an unusual mountain ridge resembles a reclining giant.

Continue along the coast on State 56 with pineapple fields lining the roadsides past Kapaa and Kealia. Near here a cane field road leads five miles up to Waipahee Falls. At the falls is a natural slide that whisks the swimmer into a crystal clear pool below.

The main route follows State Route 56 past the lovely Hawaiian villages of Anahola and Kilauea. A few more miles down the road is the famed North Shore coastline of Kauai. Hollywood, recognizing the almost unbelievable scenery of this paradise, used this area as background for such Polynesian epics as *South Pacific* and *Diamond Head.*

Approximate mileage: 45.

Best time for touring: Any season.

Terrain: Hilly, with some steep climbs.

Traffic: Heavy in tourist areas.

Historical points of interest: Waioli Mission, 1834.

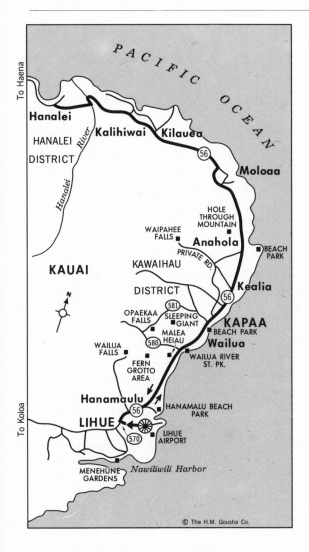

But even Tinsel Town hasn't destroyed the idyllic charm of these quiet white beaches; in fact it's even possible during the summer season to find near-deserted stretches of beach.

The route ends at the highlight of the tour. The most famous stretch along the coast, Hanalei Valley and Hanalei Bay. The other name for Hanalei is Hanohano which mean "glorious" and that's exactly what this area is. At Hanalei, visit the Waioli Mission, restored from the building constructed when the founders arrived in 1834. For the epitome of Hawaiian pleasure, you can leave your bike behind and have a helicopter take you from Hanalei and deposit your party and picnic basket on a virgin beach in the Nali Pali Coast. Afterwards, retrace the route back to the airport. Aloha.

Tour Waimea – Grand Canyon of the Pacific

A south shore tour of the island of Kauai takes the cyclist from calm sandy beaches to the majestic Grand Canyon of the Pacific—Waimea.

As you undoubtedly will fly to Kauai, begin the tour at the Lihue Airport. Take State Route 570 to the commercial and political center of the island at Lihue. One hundred years ago Lihue was just a few buildings at the heart of a huge sugar plantation. Today, it's a town marked by change, in this case the change is to tourism. But even with the rush to see this tropical wonderland, Lihue still retains its charm as a small Hawaiian village.

From Lihue the tour continues down State Route 50 past Puhi to Koloa. At Koloa there is an optional side trip to Spouting Horn and Prince Kuhio Birthplace Park. The Prince for years represented Hawaii in Washington, D.C. in Congress. At Spouting Horn waves at high tide are forced through a hole in coastal rocks to roar and burst into spectacular fountains of salt spray and foam.

Back on the route, take State 530 out of Koloa. As you cycle through the lush green foliage you will pass through the picturesque villages of Omao and Lawai.

A few miles past Lawai is the Olu Pua Gardens with food and Oriental gardens. The special treat here is the Jungle Garden, with countless shade plants and trees growing in their natural habitat.

From here the tour continues through the town of Eleele where the route takes to the beach along State Route 50. A few miles past the village of Makaweli is the Old Russian Fort. The fort was built by an ambitious member of the Russian Fur Company of Alaska who tried to claim Kauai for the mother country. Rocky ruins mark the futile effort.

At Waimea Bay is Captain Cook's landing, the first place the noted ex-

Approximate mileage: 60.

Best times for touring: Any season.

Terrain: Good highways, uphill toward Waimea State Park.

Traffic: Usually heavy.

Historical points of interest: Capt. Cook's landing place, Old Russian Fort, Prince Kuhio's birthplace.

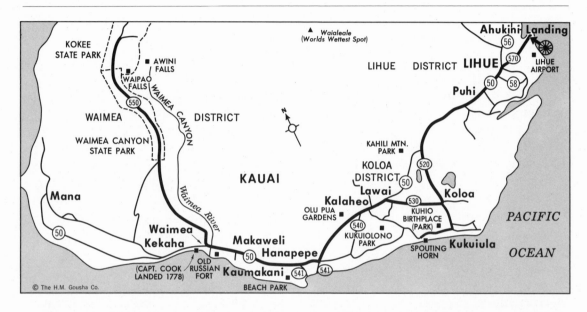

plorer set foot in Hawaii. Among people who ride funny boards in the water, Waimea is known for something besides Captain Cook. Here at certain times of the year come the largest ridable waves in the world. It's quite a sight to see these adventurers slide down the face of a forty-foot breaker.

The tour follows State Route 550 along the Grand Canyon of the Pacific, Waimea Canyon. Past the Waimea Canyon State Park the route continues through Kokee State Park to the lookout station at the base of the canyon. From here the view of the magnificent canyon and surrounding area is a fitting climax to a trip filled with scenic pleasures.

Hawaiian History Flashback in Oahu

Oahu, the true monarch of the Islands of Kings, reveals the splendor of its beaches, lush terrain and history in this 125-mile Hawaiian holiday.

There is very heavy traffic to contend with plus two-lane cliff hangers with no shoulders.

Begin the tour as soon as your bike is unloaded at Honolulu International Airport, taking State 92 (which is Nimitz Hwy. and later becomes Ala Moana).

Overlooking Waikiki is Diamond Head, the ancient crater that once served as a coast defense fort with guns poking through its high walls. Now a national landmark and state monument, the area offers spectacular vistas for the cyclist who wants to hike.

Now the route takes State 72 from Diamond Head past Maunalua Bay and Koko Head to the Halona Blow Hole.

Past Waimanalo Bay, State 72 runs into State 61. Here you have a choice: make a right turn out to Kailua and the coast or ride to the left for unforgettable views of the Pali cliffs. Pick up State 836 and make a stop at Ulu Mau Village, a flashback into Hawaiian history.

Further up the road is Laie, a settlement of Hawaiian and Samoan Mormons. An interesting landmark here is the old Mormon temple.

Also in Laie is the Polynesian Cultural Center which condenses the vast span of Polynesia with replicas of villages of Samoa, Tonga, Old Hawaii, Tahiti, Fiji and Maori New Zealand.

The back loop of the tour passes such famous surfing areas as Sunset Beach and Waimea. Past Haleiwa pick up first State 99, then State 75 and drop down to State Route 90 (Kamehameha Highway). You'll pass Pearl Harbor, significant for the December 7, 1941 bombing and subsequent U.S. involvement in World War II. Just off State 90, ride out to the *USS Arizona* Memorial Landing.

Approximate mileage: 125.

Terrain: Very mountainous with many sheer cliffs. Two-way roads with no shoulders in many places.

Best times for touring: Any season.

Traffic: Very heavy in Honolulu and around Kailua. Use extreme caution on all roads.

Historical points of interest: *USS Arizona* at Pearl Harbor, Diamond Head, Ulu Mau Village, Polynesian Cultural Center.

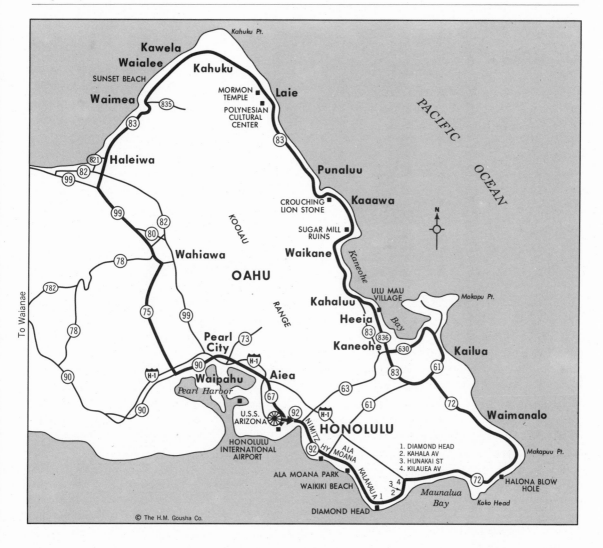

1. DIAMOND HEAD
2. KAHALA AV
3. HUNAKAI ST
4. KILAUEA AV

© The H.M. Gousha Co.

Index to Historical Points of Interest

Other Goushā Publications

☐ **LOOK TO THE MOUNTAIN TOP**

Here is a much needed overview of American Indian cultures by storytellers and scholars such as Vine Deloria, Jr., Stewart Udall, Vincent Price and Theodora Kroeber Quinn. Full color used in 70 illustrations. Paperbound . . . . $ 3.95
Clothbound . . . . $ 6.95

☐ **EXPLORER'S GUIDE TO THE WEST**

The complete guide to the famous places, the offbeat adventures, the glorious sights of The American West. Six handsome HARD COVER volumes packed in a vinyl box and accompanied by two FREE bonuses—a Wilderness Escape Map and a Prospector's Treasure Map. $12.95

☐ **AMERICAN WILDERNESS**

A complete guide to the country's Wilderness and Primitive Areas, Wild and Scenic Rivers and major trails. Each wilderness description has a map showing trails, camps, key roads. Paperbound $ 4.95

☐ **AMERICAN CRAFTS GUIDE**

A big, nationwide, comprehensive directory lists thousands of craft shops, studios, museums, galleries, supply houses, places of instruction and sources of Indian and folk art . . . . . $ 3.95

☐ **BICENTENNIAL TOURGUIDE**

Beginning with 12 activities, such as Beach Exploring, Battlefield Tours and City Touring-all with a Bicentennial theme-this atlas contains maps of all 50 states and 25 American cities; with full color photographs and maps. Paperbound . . . . $ 1.00

TOURMAPS

☐ **Rodeos**

A tourmap of America's biggest and best. Descriptions of all events. U.S. road map showing location of major rodeos. . . . . $ 1.50

☐ **Landmarks of the Revolution**

A tourmap showing all the important historical sites you can visit during the 1973-1976 Bicentennial Celebration. Detailed maps, exciting descriptions. . . . . $ 1.50

☐ **The First Americans**

A tourmap of Indian lands. Where to visit the First Americans, where to see and buy arts and crafts, and maps of ancient and modern cultures. . . . . $ 1.50

If you are unable to find any of these books locally, you can order directly from the publisher.

GOUSHA PUBLICATIONS

P.O. Box 6227   San Jose, California 95150

Allow three weeks for delivery.

63320